Power from the Margins

Power from the Margins

*The Emergence of the Latino
in the Church and in Society*

Ricardo Ramírez, C.S.B.

Bishop Emeritus Diocese of Las Cruces

ORBIS BOOKS
Maryknoll, New York 10545

ORBIS BOOKS
Maryknoll, New York 10545

Founded in 1970, Orbis Books endeavors to publish works that enlighten the mind, nourish the spirit, and challenge the conscience. The publishing arm of the Maryknoll Fathers and Brothers, Orbis seeks to explore the global dimensions of the Christian faith and mission, to invite dialogue with diverse cultures and religious traditions, and to serve the cause of reconciliation and peace. The books published reflect the views of their authors and do not represent the official position of the Maryknoll Society. To learn more about Maryknoll and Orbis Books, please visit our website at www.maryknollsociety.org.

Manufactured in the United States of America

ISBN 978-1-62698-193-5

Library of Congress Cataloging-in-Publication Data

Names: Ramírez, Ricardo, C.S.B., author.
Title: Power from the margins : the emergence of the Latino in the church and
    in society / Ricardo Ramírez, C.S.B., Bishop Emeritus Diocese of Las Cruces.
Description: Maryknoll, NY : Orbis Books, [2016] | Includes bibliographical
    references and index.
Identifiers: LCCN 2016009392 (print) | LCCN 2016014057 (ebook) |
    ISBN 9781626981935 (pbk.) | ISBN 9781608336609 (ebook)
Subjects: LCSH: Hispanic American Catholics—Religious life. | Hispanic Americans.
Classification: LCC BX1407.H55 R365 2016 (print) | LCC BX1407.H55 (ebook) |
    DDC 282/.7308968—dc23
LC record available at http://lccn.loc.gov/2016009392

To the people on the margins

with whom I have had the privilege to serve

in Mexico, Texas, and New Mexico,

and to those I have met in the existential peripheries of the world.

Contents

Foreword

Cardinal Seán Patrick O'Malley

For twenty years I worked in Washington, D.C., with immigrants from El Salvador, Guatemala, Nicaragua, and all over Latin America. The vast majority did not have the advantage of legal status. Many came to the United States in great part fleeing the violence of the civil wars in Central America.

I often share the story of my first days at the "Centro Católico" when I was visited by a man from El Salvador who sat at my desk and burst into tears as he handed me a letter from his wife back in El Salvador, remonstrating him for having abandoned her and their six children to penury and starvation.

When the man was able to compose himself, he explained to me that he came to Washington, like so many, because with the war raging in his country, it was impossible to sustain his family by farming. So a coyote brought him to Washington where he shared a room with several other men in similar circumstances. He washed dishes in two restaurants: one at lunchtime and one at dinnertime. He ate the leftover food on the dirty plates to save money. He walked to work so as not to spend any money on transportation; he could then send all the money he earned back to his family. He said he sent money each week, but now after six months, his wife had not received a single letter from him and accused him of abandoning her and the children. I asked him if he sent checks or money orders. He told me that he sent cash. He said, "Each week I put all the money I earn into an envelope with the amount of stamps that I was told and I put it in that blue mailbox on the corner." I looked out the window and I could see the blue mailbox; the problem was it was not a mailbox at all, but rather a fancy trash bin.

This incident helped me to glimpse the hardships and humiliations of so many immigrants who come to the United States fleeing from poverty and oppression, seeking a better life for their children. Sadly, many immigrants spend years without seeing their loved ones, such as when grandparents are taking care of little grandchildren because the parents are off in the United States working to send money back home.

Pope Francis encourages us to go to the periphery to seek our neighbor in places of pain and darkness. In *Power from the Margins*, Bishop Ramírez shares the fruits of a life spent in the periphery, the margins of society, where we encounter the often forgotten poor. Our immigration system in the United States is broken, and it is hurting immigrants who come to our shores in search of a better life for themselves and their children. As a nation of immigrants, we should feel a sense of identification with them, and we should work to end the suffering and pain caused by our unjust and broken immigration system.

The United States is a nation of immigrants, children of immigrants, grandchildren and great-grandchildren of people from somewhere else. Because of the potato famine and political oppression, my people came from Ireland. Thousands upon thousands perished of starvation. On the coffin ships that brought the Irish immigrants, one-third of the passengers starved. The sharks followed the ships waiting to devour the bodies of those *buried at sea.* I suspect that only the Africans brought on the slave ships had a worse passage.

Frank McCourt of *Angela's Ashes* fame wrote a play called *The Irish and How They Got That Way*. In one of the scenes, the Irish immigrants are reminiscing, saying, "We came to America because we thought the streets were paved in gold. And when we got here we discovered the streets were not paved in gold, in fact they were not paved at all, and we found out we had to pave them."

The hard work and sacrifices of so many immigrant peoples is the secret of the success of this country. Despite the xenophobic ranting of a segment of the population, our immigrant population contributes mightily to the economy and well-being of the United States.

At Lampedusa, Pope Francis warned of the globalization of indifference. Pope Francis, speaking at the borders of Europe, said,

> We have lost a sense of responsibility for our brothers and sisters. We have fallen into the hypocrisy of the Priest and Levite whom Jesus described in the parable of the Good Samaritan: we see our brother half dead on the side of the road and perhaps we say to ourselves: "Poor soul" and then go our way. It is not our responsibility, and with that we feel reassured, assuaged. The culture of comfort, which makes us think only of ourselves, makes us insensitive to the cries of other people, as if we were living in a soap bubble, indifferent to others.

Our country has been the beneficiary of so many immigrant groups that had the courage and the fortitude to come to America. They came fleeing horrific conditions and harboring a dream of a better life for their children. They were some of the most industrious, ambitious, and enterprising citizens of their own countries, and they brought enormous energy and good will to their new homeland. Their hard work and sacrifices have made this country great.

I am grateful to Bishop Ramírez for reminding me, and all those who read this book, that our immigrants are a blessing for the church and for our nation. We can learn much from them, from their values, and from their faith and traditions. There really is power from the margins, and Bishop Ramírez faithfully hands on to us what he has learned from the periphery. We are strengthened by the wisdom that we receive on the following pages.

Acknowledgments

Many people assisted in the writing of this book. I owe deep gratitude to the staff at the Institute for Latino Studies at the University of Notre Dame: Father Virgilio Elizondo; Dr. Timothy Matovina; Father Daniel Groody, C.S.C.; and Dr. Luis R. Fraga. These men inspired the concept of the book, provided professional assistance, and offered direction in their respective areas of study and specialization.

I am most thankful to Ms. Donna Curtiss, who assisted me as chief researcher and editor of the book. Ms. Debbie Moore was most helpful not only with her word processing but also with her writing skills. Ms. Velia Salinas also helped with word processing.

Among those who helped me in researching civic responsibility were Mr. Frank Sánchez and Mr. Antonio Luján. Mr. Anthony Granado, USCCB's Office of Domestic Social Development, was an invaluable resource for the section on prison and jail ministry. Father Allen Deck, S.J., provided insight with the education chapter. Mr. Federico Márquez and Dr. Christopher Adams contributed valuable information regarding the ENLACE and other Latino programs at New Mexico State University in Las Cruces. Also helpful in this regard was Mr. David Morales, the Teacher of the Year in New Mexico for 2016. Mr. Allen Sánchez, president and chief executive officer of St. Joseph Community Health, a part of Catholic Health

Initiatives, was an invaluable resource in the section on early childhood education. Dr. Ken Johnson-Mondragón, Mr. Alejandro Barraza, and Ms. Grace Cassetta were excellent sources for the chapter on Latino youth and young adults. I am grateful to Mr. Moisés Sandoval for his encouragement and advice. Father Rogelio Martínez provided invaluable insight on Aztec theology in connection with Our Lady of Guadalupe.

Soon after I began work on this project, I became quite ill and underwent two major surgeries. I can never thank Ms. Lourdes and her sister, Silvia Patricia Ramos, enough for being with me before, during, and after those surgeries. Also assisting me in my recovery was Mr. John Morales. Without these friends, I could not have undertaken and completed this project in a timely manner.

I owe my gratitude to Dr. David McNamara for reading the entire manuscript of this book and for his corrections and suggestions.

Finally, I am grateful to God for the many experiences He has provided me that served as an inspiration for this project. I am especially grateful for my early childhood experiences with my family, friends, and teachers in my hometown in Bay City, Texas, and for the education and formation I received from the Basilian Fathers at the University of St. Thomas in Houston and at St. Basil's Seminary in Toronto.

I am thankful for the ten years that I spent in Mexico studying theology and working with the poor. My time at the Mexican–American Cultural Center (MACC) in San Antonio, Texas, was a life-changing experience; there the staff and students helped me embrace and cherish my Latino heritage. Two people in San Antonio stand out as having had a special and personal influence in my life: Archbishop Patrick Flores and Fr. Virgilio Elizondo.

This book would not have been possible without the support and encouragement of Robert Ellsberg, my publisher at Orbis Books. I am grateful for his insight and recognition of the importance of the emergence of the Latino in the church and in society.

Finally, I thank God for the grace of serving the people of God in the Diocese of Las Cruces, as shepherd and missionary disciple for over thirty years.

Introduction

Most of this book was written on the eve of the Jubilee Year of Mercy, announced by Pope Francis. It is helpful to understand mercy from the Latino perspective. Mercy comes from *misericordia*, derived from two Latin words that mean misery and heart. To have *misericordia* is to feel in one's heart the misery of the other. *Misericordia* is more than just feeling sorry for someone else; it involves encounter and engagement with those who seemingly have less than us in areas such as wealth, education, health, culture, and material advantages.

I wrote this book in order to address the importance of the foundation and legacy of Latino faith, the challenges we face, and to celebrate the next generation with hope. Latino youth will carry on the faith and continue the mission of the church. It is my hope that all readers of this book, people of every ethnicity and cultural background, will gain a deeper understanding of the profound faith that lives in the Latino Catholic heart.

In this book, I share real-life experiences. As I look back, I now recognize that our small city and parish were located, physically and culturally, at the margins; yet no matter how far away we were from the mainstream, we possessed within us the fountain of life, the source of the living waters of our faith.

Over the years, through my continuous involvement with materially disadvantaged people, I have learned many things.

As a young priest, I worked in Mexico among the poorest of the poor. That experience influenced the rest of my vocation. What I discovered there was a sense of the richness that only the poor can bring to others. No matter how deep the deprivation at the margins, there are always gifts that the poor can give. The poor are not so poor that they cannot share the treasure of their faith. No one is so poor as to have nothing to offer others. Conversely, neither is one so rich that he or she cannot receive something, even from the poor.

Pope Francis, who repeatedly challenges us to go to the margins or to the periphery, and to encounter the poor, the forgotten, the ignored, and the disposable, inspires the title of this book, *Power from the Margins*.

Pope Francis, when he was Cardinal Jorge Bergoglio, was chosen to be the final editor of the Concluding Document of the Fifth General Conference of Latin American Bishops held in Aparecida, Brazil, in 2007. I was a member of the delegation from the United States. It is in the Concluding Document that we find the term *missionary disciples*. What this immediately tells us is that one cannot be a disciple of Jesus Christ without recognizing that we are missionaries, those sent to announce the joy of the Gospel.

It is the people on the margins especially who need to hear the good news of Jesus Christ. This is the primary mandate of the church—to go out of herself and reach out to those who have not yet heard the Gospel or who need to hear it once more. This is what is meant by evangelization, but evangelization is not a one-way street. We cannot think of ourselves as presenting Jesus to someone who does not know Him. Everyone, in one way or another, has a notion of goodness, love, forgiveness, mercy, and faith. They may not be able to articulate it, nor know the name of Jesus, but sometimes in mysterious ways, we discover that Jesus was already there. Therefore, for me, evangelization is the joyful encounter between the Jesus of my faith and the Jesus in the faith of the other, in the one I am evangelizing.

Repeatedly, I hear from those who minister at hospitals and prisons that they receive more from those they visit than what they give. There is power at the margins, and it is the power of the spirit of love and mercy.

As I look back at my many years of priesthood, I thank God for a lifetime of experiences of the church of the poor and the poor of the church. I reach back to my infancy and childhood in the town of my birth, Bay City, Texas. As I remember the faces of those who taught me the ways of the Gospel, I recall faces of true believers who, in good times and in bad, never lost their faith.

One person in particular stands out as a source of influence, and that was el Señor Antonio Acosta. He was the sacristan and the bell ringer, but he was more than this; he was the pillar of the faith in the community. When I went off to college he told me, "I'm so happy you're going away to study so you can come back and help us." To this day I do not fully understand what he meant by "helping us." I never returned to Bay City once I left for college, and when I became a priest, I went to el Señor Acosta and said, "I am sorry I have not helped you like you wanted me to." His answer was comforting. He said, "You don't know how much you have helped us already."

El Señor Acosta and the many others who had something to do with my upbringing were people at the margins who gave me the foundations for a life of service to others. Together with my family, they were my first teachers in the faith.

Throughout the book, I mostly use the term *Latino,* but sometimes I use *Hispanic* when quoting a source that uses that term. In my personal stories, I may use the term *Mexican–American,* when I want to refer to my specific Latino background.

Some of the chapters draw on talks, papers, and pastoral letters that I have prepared in the past, but most of the book is original and draws, as much as possible, on updated sources.

It is my hope that this book will be of special value for those involved in or preparing for Latino ministry. The ideas and practical suggestions that I offer include many I have found useful in my ministry. May they be helpful to others in their call to be missionary disciples, especially among those at the margins.

Chapter 1

La Familia in Transition

Because my parents' marriage did not work out and ended in divorce, my mother, my brother Pete, and I lived in the home of my maternal grandparents in Bay City, Texas. As is true for many people, my childhood years were among the happiest years of my life. My earliest memories include working with my grandfather in his vegetable garden. We grew carrots, cabbages, chiles, onions, and a great deal of garlic. After we had harvested many vegetables, my grandmother would send me to the store to buy a soup bone. In those days, you could buy a big chunk of bone with meat on it for twenty-five cents. The butcher would chop it into small chunks, and this was the heart of my grandmother's vegetable soup. And what wonderful soup it was! The family gathered around the table filled with food from our garden. Our home was filled with the wonderful aroma of my grandmother's fresh tortillas. My grandfather looked with joy at the fruits of his labors and exclaimed, "¡Hijos, estamos en la Gloria!" (Children, we are in heaven!).

I asked my grandfather, "Why did you plant so much garlic?" He planted row after row after row. He said, "You will see." So I tended the garden, even though it was an extra chore. When the garlic bulbs were full and ripe, we pulled them out of the garden, washed them thoroughly, and my grandfather made ristras or garlands of the garlic.

I asked him again, "Why so much garlic? Grandmother only uses so much in her soups." His answer was, "You take one to our next-door neighbor on one side of the house, and then one to the neighbor on the other side of the house. You take one to your godmother Anita." After all of the ristras, except for the one for us, were meted out, my grandfather said to me, "Now you know why we planted so much garlic." My grandfather taught me to share.

Sadness came to our home when my grandparents fell ill. When my grandfather developed skin cancer, my mother had to take him on the bus to Galveston where the nearest charity hospital was available. After checking him into the hospital, my mother did not know what to do, since she had no money or a place to stay. She simply sat on the steps of the hospital and wept. A kind Mexican–American nurse went to my mother and invited her to stay in her home. This was one of the saddest times in our lives—we could not afford to care for my grandfather. We took him home to die; sadly, we could not afford the strong painkillers. This was long before affordable health care, hospice, or Medicaid. Until his death, my mother tried to ease his pain.

Then, my grandmother got sick with diabetes, which led to blindness the last few years of her life. She later became bedridden. Again, my mother struggled to provide the best care we could afford. After my grandmother died, I thought my mother would never be happy again—that she would never recover from the loss of her parents. Then, one warm summer evening, my mother said, "Children, let's go get some ice cream." As we walked to the creamery in the middle of the empty street, my mother suddenly looked up and said "¡Miren hijos, todavía hay estrellas!" Translated, this means, "Look children, there are still stars in the sky!"

*   *   *

Our faith, our personalities, values, and lifestyles are determined early in life and in the school of the home. In the story above, one can detect elements of the traditional Latino family.

There is respect and love for the elderly and the sick, which continues in this, the twenty-first century. Whether members of the family are old or ill, or grieving the loss of a loved one, or when some are in jail or in prison, love and mercy in the family are expressed in the real terms of engaged presence with the most vulnerable.

My mother caring for her parents taught us the virtue of sacrificing our lives for others out of grateful love. In noticing the stars in the sky, she told me that God has a way of carrying us beyond pain and sorrow to the peace and serenity that come with faith-filled patience. Without having the words to say it, my mother experienced the Paschal Mystery.

Memories of early childhood and infancy either bring smiles to our faces or haunt us. In spite of the hardship of our family, most of my remembrances bring me smiles.

The United States has been home to my father's side of the family for many unknown generations, since we can trace those ancestors at least as far back as my great-grandmother, Andrea García Esquivel, who was born in New Mexico in the middle of the nineteenth century. After the Mexican–American War, the family moved from New Mexico to Brownsville, Texas. She eventually married Felipe Espitia, a Basque whose ship anchored at Port Isabel on the Gulf of Mexico. He worked as a cook on a ship, which sailed from New Orleans to Galveston, then to Corpus Christi and on to Port Isabel. My father, Natividad Espitia Ramírez, interestingly, would say our family was neither Mexican–American, nor Hispanic, nor Chicano, but *Tejano*.

I mention my father's side of the family to point out the fact that most US Latinos are not recent immigrants, nor even immigrants. Many families in the Southwest, such as those in northern New Mexico, were in what is now the United States for generations. Many can trace their ancestors back to 1620, when the first settlers arrived from Mexico, and they identify themselves, even to this day, as Spaniards. They did not move—the border did.

The Latino Family in Transition

Latino families live in a time of enormous transition, shaped by many economic and cultural factors. A consideration of the Latino family must take into account these factors—especially if we want to create programs, either in the church or through other institutions, to serve them. The role of the family in any given culture is a complex reality. This is certainly true of the Latino population. The influence of US culture and Latino families goes both ways, each impacting the other.

One of the influences the Latino population is having on US society is the way Latino influence is slowing the decline of the two-parent family. This is happening because immigration is producing a steady increase of young adults with a higher desire to marry than their native-born peers, both Latino and non-Latino.

On the other hand, the process of cultural adaptation is taking place among immigrants and their children. In other words, immigrants soon begin to take on familial attitudes similar to those of the non-Latino population, diminishing the strong sense of family among recent immigrants.

Of course, the media and popular understanding of the Latino population in the United States seem to focus on the influx of immigrants. Like my father's family, many millions of Latinos can trace their roots in the United States back many generations and reflect their own multifaceted expressions of American culture.[1]

---

[1]   Roberto Suro, "The Hispanic Family in Flux," CCF Working Paper (Washington, DC: Center on Children & the Family, Brookings Institution, 2007).

A particular concern of the Latino family in today's society is the separation of families due to immigration, military service, and incarceration. Some families separated by immigration will never again see the spouse who comes to the United States, and that spouse may eventually abandon the family in the home country to begin a new family in the United States.

Often, Latino military personnel, like others in the military, are separated for long periods from their loved ones, particularly when they are deployed to places like the Middle East. The stress experienced by the spouse left behind, having to raise the children alone, is just as difficult for the Latino family as for others. Skype and other social media are no substitute for the physical human presence of the parent.

A disproportionate number of Latinos are incarcerated in US prisons. Hispanic men are almost four times as likely to go to prison, at some point in their lives, as non-Hispanic white males.[2] According to an article in the *Huffington Post* in 2011,[3] more than half of those sentenced to federal prison were Hispanic, while Hispanics made up only 16 percent of the population.

Theological and Pastoral Concerns

The family is central to the social teachings of the Catholic Church, going back to Pope Leo XIII's historic encyclical *Rerum Novarum* in 1891. Though the central focus of that document was with the economic questions of his day, at the

---

[2] Thomas P. Bonczar and Allen J. Beck, "Lifetime Likelihood of Going to State or Federal Prison," NCJ 160092 (Washington, DC: Bureau of Justice Statistics, 1997), tbl. 9, http://bjs.gov/content/pub/pdf/Llgsfp.pdf.

[3] "Latinos Form New Majority of Those Sentenced to Federal Prison," Huffington Post (November 9, 2011), http://www.huffingtonpost.com/2011/09/09/hispanic-majority-prison_n_955823.html.

center of his analysis was the family. This is what he wrote: "The family is the 'society' of a man's house—a society very small, one must admit, but nonetheless a true society, and one older than any State. Consequently, it has rights and duties peculiar to itself which are quite independent of the State."

Ever since then, this concern for the family has been a constant feature of church teaching. The Second Vatican Council, specifically in *Gaudium et Spes,* the Pastoral Constitution on the Church in the Modern World, sent a strong message regarding the family, which is treated first, before the topics of culture, the economy, politics, or world peace. The council fathers wrote, "The well-being of the individual person and of human and Christian society is ultimately linked with the healthy condition of that community produced by marriage and the family" (no. 47).

In a talk to the Lumen Christi Conference in Chicago on April 30, 2015, my successor, Bishop Oscar Cantú, explained three key points about the family. First, because human beings are made in the image and likeness of God, they are relational, just as the Father, Son, and Holy Spirit are a community of people. To be made in God's image is to be made for community, especially the one that is most basic to humans, namely, marriage and family.

The family mirrors the Trinity, beginning with the marriage between two people who become one. Bishop Cantú states, "We are both individuals and members of a greater whole; this understanding challenges the individualism that pervades our culture. . . . When the Church emphasizes the importance of the family it does so not only because the family helps shape citizens and provides for children, but because it reflects the divine reality itself."

The family, according to church teaching, is rooted in love, not just as a sentiment, but the giving of complete self in self-sacrificing love. Moreover, as Bishop Cantú reminds us, the family is the best place suited for learning to give and receive this kind of love. It is a school for all social relationships, where we learn to live justly, gratefully sharing goods, and this lays the foundation for a civilization of love.

Practical Considerations

Latino families are typically close knit. In spite of the pressures of the host country, family ties remain strong. The term *familia* goes beyond the immediate family. In our Las Cruces area, *la familia* also refers to the extended relationships beyond parent–child relationships. Members of the extended family are cousins, aunts, uncles, grandparents, *padrinos, madrinas,* and many others whom we recognize as true members of our *familia.*

Children are highly valued in Latino families. Many times parents will not attend parties or events where their children are not welcome. Children need to feel welcomed, appreciated, or included in some way. Families celebrate all of the usual holidays, holy days, and sacraments. Celebrating a young woman's *quinceañera*, a celebration that takes place on her fifteenth birthday, denotes her transition from childhood to womanhood. The *quinceañera* is an important milestone.

Nevertheless, the family of today differs greatly from what was considered the norm or traditional family of the 1950s and 1960s, in which the father worked while the mother stayed at home to do the housework and care for the children. The old ideal involved couples marrying young, then starting a family, and staying married until death.

The family today, including the Latino family, has become more complex, and this poses many challenges to the church and society as well. Today's family might include only a single parent. More and more, we see racially mixed marriages whose children may be looked down on. There are families composed of grandparents who provide the primary care for their grandchildren as well as families where stepparents adopt the children. There are families made up of remarried spouses, each bringing to the new partnership their own children. At times, children, including school-age ones, live with their friends' families. There are many children raised in foster homes, sometimes more than one. Some families have several children from the same mother, but each has a different father. There are children of same-sex couples, adopted children, and children of teenage mothers. There are children who face special challenges, such as those who are physically or mentally disabled, or who may have one or both parents incarcerated or drug addicted.[4]

Then, there are military families who often have to move from place to place and, in some cases, with one or both parents deployed to distant lands. Tragically, sometimes a father or mother may return with physical wounds or suffering from posttraumatic stress disorder.

Among many undocumented Latinos, the family may be divided because of immigration law. A husband and father may cross the US border and become involved with another partner, disowning his original family in his country of origin. Other family considerations include some couples delaying marriage or foregoing marriage altogether. At the same time, 41 percent of children are born outside of marriage. According to the Pew Research Center, 34 percent of children today are living with an unmarried parent.[5]

---

[4]   Bishop Ricardo Ramírez, C.S.B., "The Family: Our Most Common Concern" (June 29, 1985), http://www.dioceseoflascruces.org/assets/bp_sp_72.pdf.

[5]   Gretchen Livingston, "Fewer Than Half of U.S. Kids Today Live in a 'Traditional' Family," Pew Research Center (December 22, 2014), http://www.pewresearch.org/fact-tank/2014/12/22/less-than-half-of-u-s-kids-today-live-in-a-traditional-family/.

Increasingly, two generations of adult family members may share a home. Sometimes it is so the children can care for elderly parents, and other times, the parents are there to help raise grandchildren and possibly contribute to the family's income. There are times when divorce or economic struggles result in children returning to their parents' home to live. Often times, Latinos, who place a high value on families and respect for their elders, contribute to this trend. The Pew Research Center reports that the trend is multifaceted.[6] A difficult economy, increased immigration, greater longevity, delayed marriage, and even work-life struggles are all factors in the rise of multigenerational families.

Face-to-Face Communication: An Urgent Need in Latino Families

One of the things that happens in all healthy families is that they provide a place where real communication takes place. *Ser educado*, being an educated person, means not that a person *has* a school or academic education but that the individual acquires the social skills that allow her or him to relate in a healthy way with others. A healthy family listens to everyone; people are honest and allowed to speak without interruption. A positive response from those who listen is crucial in maintaining healthy family relationships. In healthy communication, there are no put-downs or hurtful questions (e.g., "What did Johnny flunk today in school?" or "What did you burn for dinner tonight?"). I had a friend named Carlos whose father never complimented him or his brother, even when they excelled in school, in sports, or in their schoolwork. For

---

[6]   Pew Research Center, "The Return of the Multi-Generational Family Household" (March 18, 2010), http://www.pewsocialtrends.org/2010/03/18/the-return-of-the-multi-generational-family-household/.

example, Carlos would tell his dad, "I scored the most points today in the basketball game." The father, who never went to his games, would respond, "*¿Cómo estarían los demás?*" which means "the others must have been pretty bad."

In 1985, I wrote a paper entitled "The Family, Our Most Common Concern,"[7] and I believe much of what I said then is true today. For example, a healthy family is a reconciling family. We know that no family is perfect. At times, without meaning to, we hurt each other. When that happens, reconciliation needs to take place as soon as possible. We need to repair our relationships, quickly, and not carry hurt and resentment forward. Latinos frequently use the expression, "*Yo perdono pero no olvido*" (I forgive, but I do not forget). It is helpful to remember that when we forgive, it is not so much doing a favor to the one who hurt us, but it is actually doing a favor to ourselves, since we cease to allow the other person to keep hurting us.

As difficult as it may be, given our hectic lifestyles, eating dinner together is necessary for a healthy family life. Gathering around the table is a good time to update one another on what is going on in the family. My suggestion is to ban electronic devices from the family dinner table so that real communication takes place. Many families started to recognize the significance of this ritual and are setting aside time when everything outside the home is canceled at least one evening a week in order to allow the family this leisurely time together.

Healthy families provide affirmation and support. We want recognition for good things that we do. We want to feel valued by our family members. Respect is extremely important, in particular toward those who for some reason feel different from the rest of the family. Everyone should appreciate

---

[7] Ramírez, "The Family."

each family member's unique talents. Some family members may be blessed with athletic or academic abilities, others may be blessed with an ear for music or language, and still others may be the lone vegetarian in the family. Rather than make fun of the uniqueness of the individual family member, the other family members should try to understand and respect one another.

Keeping promises to other members of the family establishes and builds trust, which is an essential factor in all healthy families. Sometimes, the trust is broken and needs to be mended. I truly believe that it is a mistake to give up on someone because of a broken promise. A bad attitude can be expressed with the words, "I won't ever trust you again!" This can have disastrous results if the person saying it really means it.

Families today have become isolated; rather than watching television programs together, children have TVs and video games in their rooms; thus, sharing a movie or program together does not happen. Some of the family conversations are akin to texting today. "How was your day?" oftentimes receives a monosyllabic response, such as "fine" or "okay" or "cool." Effective communication for parents includes asking direct questions. The best times are at the dinner table or right after the school day ends. Parents should ask specific questions like, "How was the spelling test?" or "What happened today at recess?" or "What was the best thing that happened to you today?"

A healthy family teaches moral values. The worst thing parents can do in this regard is to be hypocritical. No one recognizes hypocrisy in adults better than teens. I remember a woman telling me once, "I don't know where my children get the bad words they say; they never leave the house!" Parents should not be afraid to make rules and regulations for their children. Often children appreciate the direction and concern the parents show for their moral welfare. Parents should avoid trying to be their children's best friend. As loving as they want to be, parents are still the authority in the home and must establish boundaries for the children to observe. Children themselves should be responsible for the development of their own moral principles and say to their friends, "I don't believe in doing this." In this regard, friends can be instrumental in teaching morals to one another. It is just as easy to be a good influence as it is to be a bad one.

The Synod on the Family

As this book was being written, we were between the two sessions of the Synod of Bishops on the family, with the final results yet to be seen. While traditional teachings on marriage are not expected to radically change, it is to be hoped that the synod will advocate for respect, mercy, and understanding.

In the May 4, 2015, issue of *America* magazine, Fr. Drew Christiansen, S.J., wrote an article titled, "Changing Hearts: Four Ways Pope Francis Is Transforming Church Life." Fr. Christiansen discusses humble, considerate leadership using Christ as the model of Christian leadership.

Fr. Christiansen talks about the important role bishops fulfill in caring for families. He writes, "One way to begin is to demonstrate the people's desire for dialogue with bishops on the pastoral care of families. In particular, they need to voice their desire for attention to the unexplored afflictions suffered by families outside the narrow but much ballyhooed circle of divorce, remarriage and same-sex marriage."

Concluding his article, Fr. Christiansen addresses what the church can do:

The Church can address these pastoral concerns, which include the growth of singleness among adult Catholics, single parenthood, the delay of marriage due to poverty, the emergence of combined households, violence and abuse of children and women, care for the divorced and for children of divorce, the multigenerational family and care of the infirm elderly, the impact of inequality on family strength and the spiritual growth of couples and families.

When bishops and the synod attend to these issues, then we will know today's church is advancing along the path to becoming a pastoral church.

Chapter 2

———————

Handing on the Treasure of Faith

My faith began and was nurtured in my hometown of Bay City.
The first church that our small Mexican community in Bay City used
was an old discarded railroad passenger car. The Anglo parish on the
other side of town bought the church for us, because, as explained to
me later, the parishioners did not want the Mexicans around. When
my grandparents and family arrived in Bay City, they were not
allowed in the church and had to attend Mass looking through the
windows. Later they were allowed to enter the church but had to use
the back pews. It was in that railroad passenger car that I prepared for
my First Communion.

The catechist for my First Communion was a young girl, Daría
Acosta. She taught us basic prayers and other Catholic truths, stated
in simple words, but what was lasting in our young minds was her
person. She was kind, respectful, and seemed to be happy sharing her
faith with us. She was one of those called to hand on the faith, in the
tradition of apostles, evangelizers, and catechists across the centuries.

Before Daría, my grandmother, Isidora Padrón Espinosa, called
Doña Lolita, taught me that God was up there *watching me to see*
how I behaved, and if I did anything bad, the earth would open up
and swallow me! (I was a good boy.)

14

Then there was Father William (known as Max) Murphy, a Basilian priest who came to Bay City as a newly ordained priest, whose love for catechesis was his lifelong passion. As a young boy, I was fascinated with his creative style, his humor, and his interest in us Mexican–American children. Being assigned years later to work with him in Tehuacán, Puebla, Mexico, was one of the great blessings of my young priestly life.

In Tehuacán, I joined a very creative team composed of Fr. Max and six sisters of the Missionary Catechists of the Sacred Hearts of Jesus and Mary, popularly known as Las Violetas. We noticed that at one of our parishes in Mexico, we would have at least two First Communion classes a year with about two hundred in each class. We knew something was not right because most of these children never came back to church. We agreed that it was imperative that we involve the parents in their children's faith formation.

Together the team developed a family-based program called Cate-quesis Familiar. A three-year program, it introduced the families to the basic teachings of our faith (the Father, the Son, and the Holy Spirit), the revealed Word of God (the Bible), the sacraments, and the church. When we met with the groups of parents, the most important moment was when the parents shared how during the past week they had found informal moments to talk to their children about their faith. We found that these parents, most often lower-income, blue-collar workers, were able to understand the material and, in creative ways, share that understanding of the simple verses from Scripture with their children.

To our happy surprise, through this catechetical process, a profound Trinitarian spirituality resulted. When I left Mexico in 1968 to join another pastoral team at the Mexican–American Cultural Center in San Antonio, there were approximately two thousand groups of parents using this program. To my knowledge, it still exists in some places today.

*   *   *

The key to the success of this program was due in large part to the person of Fr. Max. His Spanish was awful. Yet he managed to communicate the joy of the Gospel. Sometimes he would tell a funny story from the pulpit and he would laugh at his own story, and the whole congregation laughed with him. They did not know what he had said, they laughed simply because Fr. Max laughed. After Mass, I would ask the people, "How was it?" They would say, "It was wonderful!" I asked them, "What did he say?" Their answer was, "We don't know, but it was wonderful!" The key to his effectiveness was his love for Jesus as the Word of God and his love for the people to whom he preached.

My experience in Tehuacán with Fr. Max and the sisters left an indelible mark on my pastoral style. I especially learned from Fr. Max the three essential components of good catechesis: love of Jesus as the Word of God, love for those to whom we preach or teach, and always to be joyful in presenting the message.

Later in life, I would learn that those are the foundations as explained by St. Augustine in his treatise on catechesis, *De Catechizandis Rudibus*. In Chapter 2, he writes, "We are listened to with much greater satisfaction, indeed, when we ourselves also have pleasure in the same work; for the thread of our address is affected by the very joy of which we ourselves are sensible, and it proceeds from us with greater ease and with more acceptance. . . . What requires the greatest consideration is that everyone have pleasure in his work when he catechizes." He concludes the chapter with St. Paul's words, "For the Lord loves a cheerful giver" (2 Cor. 9:7).

The other thing that *Catequesis Familiar* taught me was that parents are the first and best catechists of their children and that the home can indeed be a *domestic church*. When we present the Word of God with joy and enthusiasm, as Pope Francis tells us, it is most effective. When the Word of God makes us joyful and enthusiastic, we cannot help but want to share it with others. Those who participated in the program wanted to share their faith with their children and then with others. Many of those who completed the three-year program went on to start other groups, which is why the numbers grew so fast. I also learned that God speaks to us from the everyday experiences of our lives, at all times and in all circumstances.

The Crisis of Catechesis Today in the Latino Community

Today's culture presents us with many obstacles to the growth of our faith. While tension between faith and reason has existed for centuries, in today's world, relativism and individualism have become the norm for both belief and action. This means there is no universal norm or objective truth. Individualism, for example, treats religion "as a private matter to be settled by each individual in the intimacy of his or her own conscience" (Cardinal Avery Dulles, S.J.). We experience challenges to our morality and our value systems never before encountered.

Living in today's society with its choices and abundance, we become vulnerable to the slick images presented by television and the press. Protests about our rights fill the media. Yet, there are no words about our obligations to love our neighbor as mandated by a life of faith. The modern media tend to dictate not only our lifestyle but also our conversation and public debates. Ours is a visual world. We buy what we see. The implication is that the unseen does not exist. This is true across cultures, including among Latinos.

A recent Pew Research study finds that the total number of Catholics in the United States dropped by three million since 2007, now comprising about 20 percent of the total population.[1] For every one Catholic convert, more than six Catholics leave the church. Catholicism loses more members than it gains at a higher rate than any other denomination, with 13 percent of the total population describing themselves as *former Catholics*. The fastest growing group is the unaffiliated or so-called nones, rising to about 23 percent of the total population from just 16 percent seven years ago.

In the light of the departure of so many US Catholics from the church, we are consoled by the fact that Latinos have added to the number of Catholics. Latino Catholics now comprise 41 percent of the US church, up six points from 2007. Immigration from Latin American countries has kept Catholic numbers stable in recent years.

Among the nones are a significant number of Latinos. In the past, we reluctantly accepted that when Latinos left the Catholic Church and joined an evangelical group, they would at least remain Christians. Now the growing tendency is that when they leave, they do not join any other religious group. Another Pew poll finds that 16 percent say they are evangelical, or *born again*, and 18 percent say they are unaffiliated.[2]

There are probably many reasons why Latinos leave the church, but what I hear often is that they do not feel the Catholic Church is feeding them God's Word. One woman told me that when she was going through her divorce, she

[1] "America's Changing Religious Landscape: Christians Decline Sharply as Share of Population; Unaffiliated and Other Faiths Continue to Grow," Pew Research Center (May 12, 2015), http://www.pewforum.org/2015/05/12/americas-changing-religious-landscape/.

[2] "The Shifting Religious Identity of Latinos in the United States: Nearly One-in-Four Latinos Are Former Catholics," Pew Research Center (May 14, 2014), http://www.pewforum.org/2014/05/07/the-shifting-religious-identity-of-latinos-in-the-united-states/.

was very distressed and needed to hear a good sermon so she went off to the Baptist church in her city and later joined that church, mainly because of the preaching.

From all this, I conclude that there is a crisis in the ministry of the Word in the church in our country. Dismal preaching pervades many of our parishes. Many priests simply do not prepare their homilies. Pope Francis is concerned about this; in his apostolic exhortation *The Joy of the Gospel* he writes, "A preacher who does not prepare is not 'spiritual'; he is dishonest and irresponsible with the gifts he has received" (*Evangelli Gaudium* no. 145). Later in the exhortation, he writes,

> If he [the preacher] does not take time to hear God's word with an open heart, if he does not allow it to touch his life, to challenge him, to impel him, and if he does not devote time to pray with that word, then he will indeed be a false prophet, a fraud, a shallow impostor. (*Evangelli Gaudium* no. 151)

Compounding the situation is that many of our preachers are from other countries and their English or Spanish is not understandable. Their English may be quite correct, but the accent is difficult and sometimes impossible to grasp. Those Catholics for whom English is not their first language, if there is no Spanish-language homily, will get nothing out of the preaching.

Our Latino communities are in dire need of bilingual preachers. Some of our Latino communities want services done in English, while others want them done in Spanish, and at times, it is convenient to do bilingual homilies. When a preacher cannot meet the linguistic needs of his parishioners (e.g., he might only know English), he could write out his homily, have it translated into Spanish, and pass out copies of it to the Spanish speakers in his congregation.

There is also a crisis in how we catechize. The rote character of *teaching catechism*, with an emphasis on checklists and rules, has been the primary model. This type of catechesis does not take into consideration the individual's faith journey, nor does it give prominence to the critical role parents play in a child's faith formation. What was true in Mexico, where children did not return after their First Communion, is true here in the United States as well. I asked a middle-school boy whether he was going to catechism. His answer was, "Oh, I'm finished with all that, I already made my First Communion." This happens also when we administer the sacrament of Confirmation.

Several years ago Dr. John Cavadini, then chair of the Department of Theology at the University of Notre Dame, in an article for *Commonweal* called, "Ignorant Catholics, the Alarming Void in Religious Education," wrote, "Perhaps the religious illiteracy of so many otherwise well-educated young Catholics is too familiar to bear mentioning again. One has come to expect that even at elite Catholic colleges and universities, entering students will not know what is meant by the 'Immaculate Conception'—hardly anyone knows that anymore. No surprise, either, when students do not know the proper number of natures and people in Christ, Mary, and the Trinity. They can speak more about re-incarnation than the Incarnation."

What are some of the causes of the crisis in catechetical instruction? I suggest that one of the major causes of the crisis is that religion is a low priority for many parents, and therefore they do not feel impelled to involve their children in the faith formation in their parish. As I stated before, First Communion seems to be a strong motivation, but once they receive First Communion, children, without the encouragement of their parents, invariably stop going to catechism.

Unfortunately, the prevalent attitude is that religious instruction is for children and young people only. Though it may seem an uphill battle, we must strive to promote lifelong learning about the faith.

We cannot expect children and young people to continue their formation in the Catholic faith if their parents do not consider their Catholicism as a priority. The surest indication of this is if they themselves are involved in adult faith formation. I cannot help but be envious of our brother and sister Protestants who have the tradition of Sunday school for all age levels. As a brother priest told me once, "Jesus used to play with the children and teach the adults, we do the opposite. We play with the adults and teach the children."

Among our Latino communities, the Cursillo movement had enormous success for a time, as did the Charismatic Renewal, and to some degree, Marriage Encounter. Nowadays the ACTS retreat (Adoration, Community, Theology, and Service) is becoming very popular in both English and Spanish parishes, at least in the US Southwest. These movements can be very successful in igniting the faith of many of our adult parishioners. There is every reason for pastoral leaders to give them all the encouragement they can. Follow-up is needed after a very inspiring weekend of conversion. The period immediately following a retreat weekend, such as those mentioned, is a great teachable moment, and participants should be channeled automatically into ongoing formation programs such as Bible study and theology.

The formation of catechists is essential. I consider them among the most important ministers in the parish, inasmuch as their teaching and witnessing give credibility to everything the church stands for and does. Years after being in faith formation, people may not remember everything they heard, but chances are they will remember their catechists and their love for Jesus and living His message. We at least owe them opportunities to develop their knowledge and skills in the transmission of the faith. Parish budgets must allow for investing in the ongoing formation of catechists. Of course, the ideal is that each parish has lay ecclesial ministers, that is, full-time catechists for both children and adults.

How Secularism Is Affecting the Church

More than ever, Americans lack confidence in organized religion. In the mid-1970s, nearly seven in ten Americans said they had a great deal of confidence in the church or organized religion. In the 1980s, the church and organized religion was number one in a Gallup survey. Today, church and organized religion ranks fourth, behind the military, small business, and the police. It still ranks ahead of the medical system, Congress, and the media.

Our society has become almost universally secular, and there is hardly any encouragement from our public schools to allow religious instruction to happen. An example is Wednesday evenings. In many places in the United States, Wednesday night was traditionally *church night*. Catholic parishes used this night to prepare young people for Confirmation and to have youth programs. With the emphasis on sports and the desire to have winning teams, coaches and other school officials have encroached into Wednesday evenings for practice, in such a way that there is no opportunity for churches to offer programs for youth. Oftentimes young people are placed in a quandary: a sports or some other event is scheduled in such a way that it conflicts with a church event, such as a Confirmation retreat, and they have to decide which of these is more important.

In our area, even Sunday mornings are no longer considered sacred. I have observed hundreds of people on Sunday morning gather in and around soccer fields where even small children are playing soccer. Among the spectators are their parents, grandparents, and friends. Unless families place importance on Sunday church observance, chances are these hundreds of people will not be attending Mass or any church service.

Sunday is no longer a day for God and for rest. It is more a time to catch up on shopping, house cleaning, and sports. Businesses remain open, and their employees and consumers do not attend church.

Transmitting the Joy of the Gospel

Pope Francis begins his apostolic exhortation *The Joy of the Gospel* with these beautiful words: "The joy of the Gospel fills the hearts and lives of all who encounter Jesus. Those who accept his offer of salvation are set free from sin, sorrow, inner emptiness and loneliness. With Christ joy is constantly born anew" (*Evangelii Gaudium* no. 1).

The Lord commanded the church to teach. She does so with the humility and confidence born from the conviction that she has received the fullness of truth in the person of Jesus Christ. She does not invent the truth. The truth has been received through divine revelation that is contained in Holy Scripture, both the New and the Old Testaments, and in the tradition of the church, which together make up one deposit of faith. From this deposit, the church draws forth the richness of faith, which she transmits through her creeds and in authoritative statements such as the writings of the papal and conciliar documents, especially in the *Catechism of the Catholic Church*, which is a sure and excellent instrument and resource to teach the faith.

Pope Francis in his *Joy of the Gospel* gives great importance to the social dimension of evangelization. The confession of the true faith has to be accompanied by commitment to help build God's Kingdom of justice and peace. By his words and actions, Pope Francis gives the highest priority to the poor in society, who must have a special place in the mind of the people of God.

The Holy Father often uses the name *missionary disciples*, a term introduced by the Latin American bishops at their Fifth General Conference in Aparecida, Brazil, 2007. Cardinal Jorge Bergoglio was the chief redactor of the final document of Aparecida, so for him, missionary disciples are an essential component of his pastoral vision. This means that we cannot be disciples without being missionaries, for a true disciple is so convinced of Jesus Christ that he cannot help but want to share that conviction with others. The sign that we have successfully transmitted the Word of God is when its hearers become its proclaimers. Catechists and preachers of the Word should always keep this idea in mind. Our aim is to bring so much excitement to our audiences that we motivate them to share that excitement.

Chapter 3

Educating with *¡Sí Se Puede!*

Where I grew up, a group of Mexican–American families, six in all, wound up living in poorly built houses in a city block isolated from other Latino families. This meant that we were all one large, extended family, whether we were blood related or not. The positive aspect to this arrangement was that we were away from some of the disadvantaged neighborhoods, such as the barrios, where violence and cantinas were more common. Among our neighbors were my padrinos or godparents, Carlos and Anita Martínez, and their son Charlie. Carlos was the only Mexican–American police officer in the city, so he was enormously respected. His son Charlie eventually was the first Mexican–American mayor of Bay City. My godmother Anita was one of the dearest people in my infancy and childhood.

Our next-door neighbors were the Acosta family, composed of twelve children whose father struggled to feed and clothe them. What was unique about the Acosta family was that they gave high priority to school. They all graduated from high school, and a few went on to college. They embraced the English language and many other things American, such as American films, music, dance, and attire. Some of them became strong role models for me.

In my case, it is true that it takes a community to raise a child. For, in addition to a supportive family who encouraged my brother and me in school, a supportive neighborhood also kept us focused on our education. We were warned frequently that if we did not go to school, we would wind up picking cotton and working for the city with "pico y pala" (pick and shovel).

Having been born in 1936, I experienced the onslaught of the Depression and World War II. The impact of the war was enormous on the psyche and lifestyle of the Mexican–American. Before World War II, Spanish was practically our only language; our food was rice, beans, chili, and tortillas; and Mexican polkas and rancheras were the music we loved to dance to. The Mexican flag was raised on September 16, Mexican Independence Day, and the Mexican National Anthem was sung. After the war, our fathers, uncles, and older brothers returned with a preference for the English language, fried chicken, mashed potatoes and gravy, and big band music; the preferred dance was the jitterbug. There was a reverence for the American flag and "The Star-Spangled Banner." I recall going to rallies where we all bought US War Bonds or savings stamps. We went out, collected scrap iron, planted Victory Gardens, and broke any little trinket made in Japan; and we began to celebrate the Fourth of July. Thus, we became Mexican–AMERICANS.

Growing up in Bay City, Texas, we Mexican–American children went to a segregated school called the Latin American School. We did not know the word segregation, *and it was actually pleasant to be with other Mexican–American children. It strikes me now that throughout the twelve years of my public school education, there were no Latino teachers or administrators in our schools. Our teachers were generally loving and kind, with the exception of Ms. Pearl Love, who was strict and wielded a mean paddle. On one occasion, I attained enough demerits to be spanked. It was the most humiliating experience of my childhood because I always tried to set an example for others. After all, I always won the spelling bee on Friday and came away with a fifty-cent piece.*

A sudden change came when we were in the middle of the sixth grade. The following week we would be going to Jefferson Davis

School, where we would mix with the Anglo children. We were scared to death, but quickly found our fears unfounded. We were treated with respect and acceptance.

When I asked my mother if I could be in the band and explained we needed to buy a musical instrument, she said we could not afford it. It was not until my senior year in high school that I joined the a cappella choir as a first tenor. It was the beginning of a lifelong love of music, especially classical. I am thankful my public school teachers were supportive and encouraging, and I knew I must go on to college.

*   *   *

Yes, there were so many incentives to go to, and stay in, school. Like all people who achieve anything in life, we know that we did not do it by ourselves. Many people helped and inspired us. In my case, there were family, neighbors, and people in the community, including the church, who influenced me. Among these was my cousin, Johnny Rico, who was part of our neighborhood extended family. He was the first in our family to graduate from high school, and he went on to become an accomplished typewriter mechanic. I admired him because he went to work in dressy clothes and came back just as clean. As a child, I thought to myself, "I want to do what Johnny does; I want to be a typewriter mechanic." That was the first of my aspirations.

I recall one instance with my grandmother when I was a toddler. There were no writing tools available at home except for a pencil. I recall being on the floor with the pencil and writing on the margins of a newspaper. I say "writing," but it was actually scribbling that formed no letters or words. I shouted to my grandmother, "Grandma! I know how to write!" My grandmother simply answered, with a twinkle in her eye, "That's wonderful, son."

One of my favorite memories is of a gift I received at church. Since we were a poor mission of the Basilian Fathers, a large, wealthy parish in Houston would send us wrapped Christmas presents. Each one had a label, indicating the appropriate age group and sex of the potential recipient. One Christmas I received a present with a gift tag, "To a young boy." To my delight, it was a book. It was the first book I ever owned, and it was *Grimms' Fairy Tales*. I read and reread every story and treasured the book for years. What that book did was to whet my imagination and begin my lifelong love of books and reading.

The Reality of Education among Latinos

Because family environments, including among Latinos, have deteriorated over the past forty years, a growing number of our children are born into disadvantaged families. James Heckman, in the book *Giving Kids a Fair Chance,* states, "The accident of birth is a principal source of inequality in America today. American society is dividing into skilled and unskilled, and the roots of this division lie in early childhood experiences. Kids born into disadvantaged environments are at much greater risk of being unskilled, having low lifetime earnings, and facing a range of personal and social troubles, including poor health, teen pregnancy, and crime. While we celebrate equality of opportunity, we live in a society in which birth is becoming fate."[1]

In the same book, Annette Lareau talks about the role discrimination plays in the lives of children: "Two babies born today in America may have very different life chances depending on the social class of their parents." The baby born to edu-

---

[1] James J. Heckman, *Giving Kids a Fair Chance* (Cambridge, MA: MIT Press, 2013).

cated parents will be read to, driven to extracurricular activities, and urged to attend college. The baby born at the edge of economic survival will not enjoy those advantages.

Children in advantaged homes, regardless of their cultural group, benefit from cognitive and financial resources. Steady employment and a stable home environment are contributing factors to a child's educational and overall achievement in life. Robert D. Putnam, in his book *Our Kids: The American Dream in Crisis,*[2] states, "Kids from more affluent homes are exposed to less toxic stress than kids raised in poverty."

Today, disadvantaged children are missing so much more than material wealth. Too many children suffer childhood hunger and food insecurity, which means they do not know when the next meal will come. "Childhood hunger steals opportunities and dims futures," says Bill Shore, founder of Share Our Strength. Although children from low-income families qualify for a free or reduced-price breakfast at school, ten million eligible kids do not receive the food because of the stigma attached, or turbulence in their home lives, prevents them from getting to school on time to enjoy breakfast.

Children who grow up in fractured families and isolated situations lead to a grim economic picture for our nation. Pope Francis tells us it is an "injustice" to isolate the young as though their needs and their pain "were someone else's responsibility and not our own." These children have caught the attention of our nation's leadership.

"The idea that so many children are born into poverty in the wealthiest nation on Earth is heartbreaking enough," President Obama declared. "But the idea that a child may never be able to escape that poverty because she lacks a decent education

---

[2] Robert D. Putnam· *Our Kids: The American Dream in Crisis* (New York: Simon & Schuster, 2015).

or health care, or a community that views her future as their own, that should offend all of us."[3]

In 2011, President Barack Obama recognized, "At more than fifty-four million strong, including nearly four million in Puerto Rico, Latinos constitute the country's largest and fastest-growing minority group. Latinos had a profound as well as a positive impact on our country through, among other things, their community's strong commitment to family, faith, hard work, and service."

The Latino population was projected to increase from 55 million in 2014 to 119 million in 2060, an increase of 115 percent. In 2014, Latinos were projected to account for 17 percent of the US population. By 2060, the Latino US population is projected to be 29 percent—more than one-quarter of the total population.

Despite the growth in the Latino population, US Latinos have the lowest education attainment levels. Latino students face persistent obstacles to educational attainment. Fewer than half of Latino children enroll in any early learning program. Only about half of all Latino students earn their high school diploma on time; those who do complete high school are only half as likely as their peers to be prepared to go on to college. Thirteen percent of Latinos have a bachelor's degree, and only 4 percent complete graduate or professional degree programs.[4]

There are programs in place in the Catholic and public school systems that seek to address higher attainment levels. Some successful programs are discussed in the following sections.

---

[3] Remarks by the President on Economic Mobility, White House press release, December 4, 2014, https://www.whitehouse.gov/the-press-office/2013/12/04/remarks-president-economic-mobility.

[4] US Department of Education and White House Initiative on Educational Excellence for Hispanics, "Winning the Future, Improving Education for the Latino Community" (April 2011), https://www.whitehouse.gov/sites/default/files/rss_viewer/WinningTheFutureImprovingLatinoEducation.pdf.

Catholic Schools' Innovative Programs

Fr. Osmar Aguirre, a priest in the Diocese of Yakima, Washington, recently completed a doctoral dissertation that provides an important framework for understanding the importance of educating second-generation Latino youth.

Fr. Osmar says that, for best results, Catholic schools need to develop strategies that will help young Latinos interpret their story from the perspective of what God is doing here and now in their communities, and how their lived experience can be a real occasion of grace for themselves and the entire church. From a faith perspective, this reflection is enhanced by a clear proclamation that the experiences of marginalized people have been a paramount source of divine grace throughout salvation history.[5]

The Jesuit Schools Network does that. The Jesuit high schools initiate programs and provide services that enable the Jesuit Schools Network member schools to sustain their Ignatian vision and Jesuit mission of educational excellence in the formation of young men and women of competence, conscience, and compassion.

The Cristo Rey High Schools

Recognizing that Catholic education is among the richest treasures in the US church, innovative programs have arisen that offer the opportunity of Catholic education to underserved children and young people. These programs also assist dioceses and parishes with the financial challenges that many of our Catholic schools are facing.

---

[5] Osmar Aguirre, "Following Jesus Christ to the Margins: Understanding and Evangelizing Second-Generation Latino Youth in the United States" (PhD diss., Pontifical Gregorian University, 2012).

First, there is the Cristo Rey High School Network. Students at Cristo Rey High Schools follow a model whereby they work five days each month in an entry-level job at a professional company. The pay they receive underwrites their tuition costs. The idea for these schools, which first began in Chicago, came from the missionary experience of Fr. John P. Foley, S.J., who spent thirty-four years working in education in Tacna, Peru. This successful model provides an affordable alternative for urban families who seek a small, Catholic, college preparatory school for their daughters and sons. In 2015, there were 30 Cristo Rey High Schools nationwide with 9,955 students enrolled and 9,825 alumni. The average income of families served by these schools was $35,000. In all, in 2015, there were 2,325 corporate partners and 40 religious sponsors and endorsers. This network serves Latino high school students preparing for college.

The Nativity and San Miguel Schools

Two religious teaching congregations, the Jesuits and the Christian Brothers, saw the need to educate middle school-age children, especially in inner cities where significant numbers of Latinos reside.

The Jesuits began a middle school in the Lower East Side of Manhattan to serve the waves of Dominican and Puerto Rican immigrants settling in the area. The school had an extended school day. Attendance nearly doubled that of the local public school. A low student-to-teacher ratio ensured time for one-on-one instruction, and a summer academic program extended learning the year round. A unique aspect of the concept was to support their graduates through high school and guide them on to college. The model spread to other cities so that by 2015 there were nineteen of these schools.

The Christian Brothers began their first San Miguel middle school in Providence, Rhode Island, in 1993, and it, too, gained the attention of Catholic educators in other places. By 2015, there were twenty of these schools throughout the United States.

In 2006, both networks merged to form the Nativity Miguel Network of Schools. Some are all male, some all-female, and others coeducational. Although the network ceased to exist in 2008, another coalition of the Nativity Miguel Schools was formed in 2012. In 2015, there were fifty schools in the coalition. The tradition of offering ongoing support to their alumni continues even into college.

The University of Notre Dame Alliance for Catholic Education (ACE)

The Alliance for Catholic Education at the University of Notre Dame, generally known as the ACE concept, has sought for more than twenty years to strengthen and transform Catholic education in the United States and beyond our borders. Its aim is that Catholic schools continue to provide an education of the highest quality to as many children as possible, especially disadvantaged children.

In 2015, one in four Catholic schools in the United States were assisted by ACE. It has spread to 70 percent of the US dioceses and has formed 2,000 teachers and leaders affecting 180,000 students. Many of these are Latino children and youth.

ACE incorporates several programs. The ACE Teaching Fellows is the foundational program; it is the nation's largest program forming talent specifically for Catholic elementary and secondary schools. It combines an intensive schedule of academic classes, held during the summer at Notre Dame, with two years of applied learning, teaching in classrooms in underresourced Catholic schools. Academic preparation combines with community-building and spiritual growth. This program supports approximately 180 teachers in more than 100 elementary and secondary Catholic schools in over 30 cities each year. ACE teachers live in community houses in their apprenticeship areas.

In 2008, the University of Notre Dame commissioned the Notre Dame Task Force on the Participation of Latino Children and Families in Catholic Schools. The task force report, "To Nurture the Soul of a Nation," was published on the Feast Day of Our Lady of Guadalupe in December 2009. The report revealed that at that time Latinos represented approximately 70 percent of all practicing Catholics under the age of thirty-five, yet only 3 percent of school-age Latino children were enrolled in Catholic schools. This was a regrettable fact considering that Latino children are 40 percent more likely to graduate from high school and more than twice as likely to graduate from college when they attend K–12 Catholic schools.[6]

Given that the vast majority of Latino young people attend public schools, there is also much work to do in this area. The programs below are just a couple of those having a positive impact on the lives of Latino young people.

Secular Education's Innovative Programs

ENgaging LAtino Communities in Education (ENLACE)

In 2000, the Kellogg Foundation, alarmed by the school dropout rate and other negative trends among Latino chil-

---

[6] University of Notre Dame Task Force on the Participation of Latino Children and Families in Catholic Schools, "To Nurture the Soul of a Nation: Latino Families, Catholic Schools and Educational Opportunity" (2009), https://ace.nd.edu/files/ACE-CSA/nd_ltf_report_final_english_12.2.pdf.

dren, in collaboration with educators, including Latino teachers, studied ways of dealing with this crisis. Kellogg wanted to fund projects that would be practical and successful in bringing Latino students along. ENLACE eventually was active in a number of states, especially those with a high-density Latino population, such as California, Arizona, New Mexico, Texas, Florida, and the cities of Chicago and New York. Each state developed its own application of certain core principles, such as community, family, and educational institutions, to collaborate in successfully guiding students to enroll at the college level and continue until obtaining a degree.

All ENLACE programs and projects focus on raising literacy levels, and increasing academic planning and achievement. After the Kellogg grant was completed, New Mexico continued funding ENLACE at the university level. The university provides resources to area high schools. The public school district provides classrooms and teachers. A core curriculum has been developed by ENLACE and is revised annually to reflect the cultural needs.

Under the directorship of Dr. Federico Márquez of New Mexico State University (NMSU), the Southern New Mexico ENLACE Collaborative begins by engaging parents of elementary school children and follows through to the students' first year of college. The result has been a 100 percent retention rate among first-year college students.

Mr. David Morales, Teacher of the Year in the state of New Mexico for 2016 and ENLACE teacher for Mayfield High School in Las Cruces, says this about the program:

> The most important way to reach Latino students is to have their educational experience culturally reflected. The Latino culture is family-centered. When you establish that in a classroom, it makes all the difference. Stu-

dents hold each other accountable, even more than I do. They know that what each of them accomplishes reflects on all of them.

At Mayfield High School, Latino youth are interviewed for admission to the program. The current class interviews prospective classmates, and they look for those who need the program. As a result, there are students who are academically accomplished and those who are academically challenged. "It works for us," says Morales.

At NMSU in Las Cruces, students entering the freshman class attend an ENLACE class called EXITO, which helps students acclimate to college and connects them with mentors and professors in their chosen field of study who will be available to help and guide them throughout their college experience.

The ENLACE program in New Mexico has assisted 35,000 students statewide and served 6,548 students in direct service programs. Most importantly, ENLACE achieved a 97 percent high school graduation rate and demonstrated a 95 percent grade-to-grade matriculation rate. ENLACE has also maintained a 98 percent program retention rate.

College Assistance Migrant Program (CAMP)

CAMP is a federally funded program to help migrant or seasonal farmworkers' children attend college. The goal of CAMP at NMSU is to ensure that each CAMP student graduates from NMSU with a bachelor's degree. CAMP offers the first line of support for CAMP students to succeed during the first year at the university. CAMP also strives to maintain communication with former students to guarantee that they receive the support needed in order to graduate from NMSU.

CAMP's peer mentoring program, the COMPAS Program, matches students with program alumni at least once a week. The mentoring program offers students activities that include tutoring, cultural events, workshops, and exploring campus resources. The goal is to foster lasting friendships that benefit both the mentor and the student.

CAMP was recognized by the White House as a "Bright Spot in Hispanic Education" in 2015. The Bright Spots initiative seeks to encourage sharing data-driven approaches, promising practices, and effective partnerships that result in increased support for educational attainment of Latino youth. "Our students are proving how successful we are by landing jobs in their fields of expertise," said Cynthia Bejarano, principal investigator of the program she founded. "We have accountants, CPAs, engineers, and teachers who are working in New Mexico and elsewhere—Texas, Indiana, California, and Ohio."

For the 2013–2014 academic year, all twenty-nine freshmen enrolled in the program successfully completed their first year with a combined cumulative grade point average of 3.1. The academic year ended with twenty CAMP students earning a bachelor's degree, four CAMP students receiving their master's degree, and one earning a PhD—a record number for the CAMP program. Since the inception of CAMP at NMSU in 2002, 319 students have participated in CAMP, and 105 students have earned a degree.

The Urgent Need for Early Childhood Education among Latinos

The years prior to kindergarten are among the most significant in shaping a child's foundation for learning and school success. Research shows that learning begins at birth and takes shape as children are nurtured, challenged, and engaged in high-quality learning environments and in relationships with parents and other caregivers.

Compared to other minority groups, Latino children represent the largest segment of the early childhood population in the nation, but they are less likely than any other group to enroll in early education programs. By age two, Latino children are less likely than their non-Latino peers to demonstrate expressive vocabulary skills. Preschool-age Latino children also exhibit lower average scores in language and mathematics knowledge than their non-Latino peers.

Though educators agree that early childhood education is important in the educational development of young children, it is not mandated. There are many reasons why young children do not attend pre-K; many times poverty plays a role in that the families do not have the resources needed to send their young children to preschool.

Not attending pre-K puts children at a disadvantage in this early stage of life when they need exposure to learning to increase their vocabularies. They need to develop social skills. Not attending puts young children at a disadvantage when they enter kindergarten and begin their education behind their peers. When young children enter kindergarten not knowing how to express their feeling and thoughts, not able to interact socially with the other children, the achievement gap widens. So long as pre-K remains optional, many of our children will miss the opportunity to develop a true love of learning at a time when their minds are ready and willing to learn.

Disadvantaged children who gain access to such programs, from birth through age five, are more likely to improve their cognitive, social, emotional, and language development. Later effects of high-quality programs to improve academic achievement reduce the need for special education, increase employment and earnings, reduce crime and delinquency, and ultimately increase international competitiveness.

James J. Heckman writes,

Our nation faces significant economic and social challenges. Investing in quality early childhood education for disadvantaged children is an important component of a strategy for developing skills that help people thrive and society prosper. It is socially fair and economically efficient. A few essential principles, include focus on disadvantaged families, start at birth, integrate health, develop cognitive and character skills, and encourage local innovation in quality programs from birth to age five.

What One Person Can Do

In the state of New Mexico, the child poverty rate rose to 31 percent, using 2013 data. The *Kids Count Data Book* published in 2015 by New Mexico Voices for Children, with grant funding from the Annie E. Casey Foundation, ranks New Mexico forty-ninth in child well-being. "Over the last several years, we've seen 38,000 children fall into poverty in New Mexico," said Dr. Veronica C. García, EdD, Executive Director of New Mexico Voices for Children. "That is simply not acceptable." Dr. García goes on to say that ensuring children have the high-quality care and learning experiences in the early years to support robust brain development, ensuring doctor's care, nutritious food, and providing for schools and educators are ways to meet some of their basic needs.

One wonderful example of meeting basic needs and, in this case, exceeding basic needs is the work of Sonya Romero-

Smith, a kindergarten teacher in Albuquerque, New Mexico. Her story first appeared in the *Washington Post* in an educational piece titled "Majority of US Public School Students Are in Poverty."[7] The article reported that for the first time in at least fifty years, a majority of US public school students come from low-income families. According to the federal data released in 2015, 51 percent of students in pre-K through twelfth grade in the 2012–2013 school year were eligible for free and reduced-price lunch.

The *Washington Post* quoted Ms. Sonya Romero-Smith, a veteran teacher at Lew Wallace Elementary School in Albuquerque, "When they first come in my door in the morning, the first thing I do is an inventory of immediate needs: Did you eat? Are you clean? A big part of my job is making them feel safe." Fourteen of her eighteen kindergartners are eligible for free lunches. She helps them clean up with bathroom wipes and toothbrushes, and she stocks a drawer with clean socks, underwear, pants, and shoes.

Romero-Smith, a teacher for nineteen years, became a foster mother in November to two girls, sisters, who attend her school. They had been homeless, their father living on the streets and their mother in jail, she said. When she took the girls into her home, the disarray of their young lives shocked her.

"Getting rid of bedbugs took us a while. Night terrors, that took a little while. Hoarding food, flushing a toilet, and washing hands, it took us a little while," she said. "You spend some time with little ones like this and it's gut wrenching. . . . These kids aren't thinking, 'Am I going to take a test today?' They're thinking, 'Am I going to be okay?'"

---

[7] Lyndsey Layton, "Majority of US Public School Students Are in Poverty," *Washington Post* (January 16, 2015), https://www.washingtonpost.com/local/education/majority-of-us-public-school-students-are-in-poverty/2015/01/15/df7171d0-9ce9-11e4-a7ee-526210d665b4_story.html.

The Role of the Church

The church has long recognized that parents are the first and most important teachers in their children's lives. Parents have the primary responsibility for educating their children. This is why it is so essential for parents and teachers to work together. Parents provide a vibrant home environment where faith and education grow together for all members of the family. The task of teachers is to continue to provide the same environment, one in which teaching and learning thrive. Further, parishes and communities play a supportive role.

In an article in the *Catholic Telegraph* (newspaper of the Archdiocese of Cincinnati), Jim Rigg, superintendent of Catholic schools, states, "True evangelization for children only works when parents work in partnership with educators and are complemented by parishes that are vibrant, reliant, and welcoming."

What the local churches can do is to support Catholic schools and to give special consideration for a preschool program in the parish. This can be done in parishes that cannot, for financial reasons, have a parochial school. Parishes can invest in educational and developmental resources for disadvantaged families to provide equal access to successful early childhood development.

The church can provide consistent family support, which is imperative for the emotional, educational, physical, and spiritual growth of a child. Total success comes from community support, specifically when the family, school, and community work together.

For centuries, the church has been involved in the education of the human being, from the medieval universities to the parochial school system in the United States. Although parochial schools are experiencing challenges, they can still be effective vehicles for delivering early childhood education and an education that builds a genuine relationship with Jesus Christ into every aspect of the school curriculum.

Community Support

Earlier in this chapter, I recounted that it takes a community to raise a child. The strengths of family, extended family, school, and community support are all important to our children's future. Providing a nurturing environment for our children is a wonderful opportunity to create better outcomes for the children and for their families.

Children need to know they are loved and valued, and that they belong. Having friends, family, neighbors, and teachers provide emotional support is important for the child as well as the family. Finding community support is a little more difficult to identify because community takes such differing forms. All communities have distinct advantages and disadvantages. Communities can be rural and isolated, and associated with persistent high percentages of poverty. For example, New Mexico is the fifth largest state in square miles; it ranks thirty-sixth in population, which means the state's rural communities are more geographically isolated than in most states, making access to education and family support more difficult. Inner-city communities can be isolated in a different way. At times, there are gang members, drug dealers, and other forms of street violence. Community may also take the form of suburbs, villages, and small or large cities.

Today, just as in my childhood, family, school, church, and community involvement is the best way to protect and educate our children successfully. Support might come from extended family and neighbors, as happened for my brother and me. Close friends oftentimes become adopted family, an extended family of our own choosing, and they are able to provide encouragement and support to the children. This happens frequently in military families. Whatever form the community takes, it is important to know your neighbors. Many people create lifelong friendships by getting to know the next-door neighbor.

My hope and prayer are that in reading this chapter the reader will come away with validation of the importance of education and the roles we all play in the life of every child. It is my belief that when children have the love of family, supported by community, we give them the best childhood possible. When we are able to do that, the entire community succeeds.

Chapter 4

Latino Youth:
Joy of Today, Hope for Tomorrow

Growing up as a Mexican–American in Bay City in the 1940s and 1950s, the years of my youth, had its challenges. Bay City is located in the heart of the Texas Gulf Coast; as such, it is at the western edge of the Deep South. Much of the racism that characterized the Deep South was, and still is, to some degree, the milieu in which I grew up. The African Americans had their part of town together with their own segregated schools (separate and incredibly unequal). In chapter 3, I described the Latin American school where Mexican–American children attended the first six years of elementary school. Restaurants or soda fountains did not allow people of color. During the summer, we used the municipal swimming pool only on Friday—the day before they changed the water.

The town was divided into three groups: the Anglos, the African Americans, and the Mexican–Americans. There were three separate schools, three places to sit in the movie theaters and other public places such as the bus station, three water fountains at the courthouse, and three places to sit on the bus and train. While I was in high school, members of the student council went to the movies for free. I was the only Mexican–American member, and I was in a quandary: where should I sit? I did not want to go against the rules by sitting in the Anglo section of the movie house. I finally decided to sit in the Mexican side with a Mexican–American buddy.

Attending school with Anglos allowed us to get to know each other across ethnic and cultural lines. Extracurricular activities, such as sports and music programs, brought us together. At the same time, however, outside of school, there was little social interplay among us; our socializing stopped when we left school.

Within the confines of our Mexican–American world, we had enjoyable and exciting times, and much of our lives centered on our parish, which at that time had the name Our Lady of Perpetual Help Church. We belonged to a Catholic Youth Organization (C.Y.O.) and planned activities throughout the year. We had celebrations at Halloween, Christmas, and Valentine's Day, and beach parties in the summer. We helped at bazaars and fiestas. For a while, we organized holy hours; surprisingly, these were well attended. Most of the C.Y.O. members made up the parish choir. With my limited knowledge of music, I was the choir leader. I must admit, however, that Gregorian chants posed a formidable task for us, and we stumbled through the Missa de Angelis.

*   *   *

The remarkable part of this story is that there was little adult leadership in our youth community. It helped that we were a tightly knit group, caring and watching out for each other, wanting to enjoy life in healthy and simple ways. Most of us did not own automobiles, and so we walked everywhere—we got our exercise. The pastor, Father Joe Shannon, C.S.B., gave us the freedom to do the things we did. Our parents were encouraging and trusting. As in my infancy, my young years as a teenager were generally happy, and the church had a lot to do with this. Our small Mexican–American parish was a real community where we young people found great support and encouragement.

When a person grows up in a racially and culturally divided ambience, the effect on one's self-image can be extremely negative. Children and young people of a minority group are often reminded that they are not only different from those of the majority group but that they are inferior. This happened in my case. My *mestizo* self as a Mexican and an American made me feel inferior in two ways: I felt that I was not a real Mexican, and at the same time, I felt like a lesser American. When my studies and priestly ministry took me to Mexico, it caused me to think that I was like a ping-pong ball: not totally accepted as an American in the United States or fully accepted as a Mexican in Mexico.

It was not until I went to the Mexican–American Cultural Center (MACC) in San Antonio, Texas, that I began to appreciate my double identity. Listening to Fr. Virgilio Elizondo, founder and president of MACC, present a theological approach to *mestizaje,* and discovering the history, literature, and cultural expressions of Chicanos and Mexican–Americans, I recognized the richness of my Mexican–American heritage. It was a moment of grace for me. As a Mexican, I was part of a rich culture that most Americans could not claim. As an American, I had an equally valuable background that most Mexicans did not share. I could finally thank God that I was a Mexican–American. Deep in my heart, I was convinced that God loved me as much as He loved anyone else.

We grew up with a Catholic culture in Bay City. Most of our Mexican–American peers were Catholics. Only one family went to the Presbyterian church. We took for granted that we would continue the faith of our fathers and mothers. Our Catholic faith bound us together. Even though over time we went our separate ways, we still consider ourselves as lifelong friends, and when we do see one another, it is a time of exceeding joy.

Two things stand out as the most formative in my dual identity as Mexican and American. When I went to Mexico, I was around twenty-five years old. My Mexican–American culture was evident in the language that I spoke. I always thought that I knew Spanish well, but when I went to Mexico, people there laughed at the Spanglish that was my first language—neither pure Spanish nor English. When some of my Mexican seminarian friends called me "el gringo," I vowed I would learn Spanish and would speak the language correctly. One of the methods I used was reading the daily newspaper with a Spanish–English dictionary nearby. It also helped that I studied the last two years of theology at the *Seminario Conciliar de México*. For the first time in my life, I was forced to read theology and write papers in Spanish.

I left Mexico in 1966 after I was ordained a priest but returned after graduate studies in 1968. I remained in Mexico as a missionary for the next eight years. During those years, I came to love my Mexican background and studied as much of the history and the literature as I could get my hands on. I remember one day standing in the middle of the *Zócalo*, the major plaza in the center of Mexico City, with the National Cathedral on one side and government buildings on the other three sides. With deep emotion, I experienced the fascinating story of the Mexican people and felt immensely proud to be part of it all. I experienced an equivalent feeling when I visited Washington, DC, for the first time and sat in the observers' balcony in the Capitol in the House of Representatives and watched democracy at work. There, I felt the pride of being an American. What developed gradually in my sense of self took years, and I am sure that other people with similar, dual or multiple backgrounds must experience the same feelings of patriotism and belonging.

Challenges in the Formation of Children of Immigrants

In the previous chapter, I mentioned the dissertation by Fr. Osmar Aguirre. His work, *Following Jesus Christ to the Margins: Understanding and Evangelizing Second-Generation Latino Youth in the United States*, provides an important framework for understanding the theological and pastoral significance of ministry with US-born Latino adolescents.[1] He begins by naming the problem in ways reminiscent of my own experience.

> Latino immigrant parents see themselves vividly present in the lives of their children. . . . Their reason for living comes from the ability to provide adequate nurturance, with the hope of shaping them into productive adults who appreciate themselves and others. Thus, being raised with these values, the second-generation Latino youth should be prone to adopt this manner of thinking. However . . . many complexities impede them from reaching their fullest potential. As a result, it can destine them and their offspring to a continuous state of poverty and marginalization with underdeveloped tools for fulfillment.
>
> This is elicited and visible in the lack of personal investment towards their human capital, which paradoxically goes against the continual search for the

---

[1] Osmar Aguirre, "Following Jesus Christ to the Margins: Understanding and Evangelizing Second-Generation Latino Youth in the United States" (PhD diss., Pontifical Gregorian University, 2012).

better way of life their parents first sought to find in this country. . . . In parish life one finds that many of these youth are lacking in academic commitment, success, and participation in the life of their Church's communities.

Fr. Aguirre goes on to explain that because the life issues they are experiencing are substantially different from those faced by either the immigrant Latino youth or the US-born teens of the mainstream culture, lumping them together in a pastoral setting is not the most suitable approach. Their spirits need feeding in a way that responds to the particular cry of the US-born (or raised) Latino/adolescent: "¡No soy de aquí ni de allá!—I'm neither from here nor from there!" That cry for belonging is really a search for community and identity—two historical hallmarks of Catholic life—so it is particularly tragic that "the U.S. Church has failed to make the second-generation Latino youth a missionary pastoral priority."

The key to a renewed pastoral outreach to second-generation Latino youth lies in helping them to understand the beatitude that lies in their experience of social and religious marginality:

Marginalized and poor people can discern and develop spiritual qualities and values that help them transcend their physical suffering and despair. The proper encounter with the reality of marginality can become a vehicle for conversion and transcendent liberation for everyone in the society. The dynamic of recognizing and appreciating one's true identity in God, which is coupled by obedience, trust, and even suffering, leads toward the realization of a transcendental vocation of service. . . .

Jesus dignified and legitimized the marginalized and poor, as he chose them to be the ongoing revelatory encounters of his presence. Therefore, in actively encountering the world of the marginalized people, one is entering into the potential locus of God's dynamic force that transforms and redeems the world.

Working on identity issues with Latino youth begins at home. It is important for children to know their roots. Speaking in Spanish at home is crucial so that children not only understand Spanish but also are instilled with pride in being bilingual. Being multilingual is an asset in today's global economy—and it is a skill worth supporting and developing, according to experts. Celebrating Latino traditions fosters bicultural identity so that they may be successful in both cultures.

Latino Youth Ministry

Much is lacking in the US Catholic Church with regard to youth and young adult ministry, and it is markedly lacking among Latinos. The dropout rate from the church is alarming. For example, roughly one-half of Catholic teenagers lose their Catholic identity by their late twenties.[2]

In 1987, the United States Conference of Catholic Bishops (USCCB) made a commitment to a preferential missionary option in favor of service to the poor and the young in Hispanic ministry.[3] Nonetheless, the conclusion of the *First*

---

[2] Nicolette Manglos-Weber and Christian Smith, "Understanding Former Young Catholics: Findings from a National Study of American Emerging Adults," University of Notre Dame, https://icl.nd.edu/assets/170517/icl_former_catholics_final_web.pdf.

[3] United States Conference of Catholic Bishops, *National Pastoral Plan for Hispanic Ministry* (Washington, DC: Office of Publishing and Promotion Services, USCCB, 1987).

National Encounter for Hispanic Youth and Young Adult Ministry in 2008 found "most mainstream Catholic youth ministry programs in the US are reaching only a small segment of young Hispanic Catholics. Programs directed specifically to Hispanic *jóvenes* are both few in number and limited in both scope and depth."[4]

Dr. Ken Johnson-Mondragón is the director of Latino Research and Development for RCL Benziger. He is an expert in the field of Hispanic youth and young adult ministry in the Catholic Church. His research shows that Latino children comprise nearly half of all Catholics under the age of eighteen in the United States. Six years ago, it was over 50 percent foreign born, so the trend is definitely moving toward a stronger second-generation representation among Hispanic young adults. The youngest Latinos in the United States today are predominantly the children of immigrants, who will experience growing up between two cultures. Children of immigrants predominate among the teens. But there are significant differences within the population of Latino youth, which must affect our approach to ministry. Dr. Johnson-Mondragón identifies four categories: immigrant workers, identity seekers, mainstream movers, gang members and high-risk youth.

Immigrant workers are mostly Spanish speaking, of Mexican origin, and many are undocumented. About 74 percent are Catholic and seek moral and spiritual support from the church. They are interested in forming peer groups. With little formal education, larger families, and a strong work ethic, they are incredibly motivated.

Identity seekers are mostly bilingual, born in the United States, and children of immigrants. They struggle to graduate from high school and find hope in family. Some are involved

---

[4] United States Conference of Catholic Bishops, *Conclusions: First National Encounter for Hispanic Youth and Young Adult Ministry* (Washington, DC, 2008).

in alcohol abuse, drugs, or sexual promiscuity. Their self-esteem is low, and they can become unmotivated and apathetic.

Mainstream movers consist mostly of English speakers who were born in the United States. Some will go to college, especially those who attend private schools. Most of them will leave the Catholic Church. These are in the middle–upper economic level and look down on other Latinos.

Born mostly in the United States, *gang members and high-risk youth* live in the low economic levels. They tend to live in inner cities, are unemployed, and may become drug/alcohol users/sellers. Many are angry at society, experience despair, and wind up incarcerated. They may be involved in special church programs.

Responding to the Diversity among Latino Youth

Ms. Grace Cassetta, Director of Youth Ministry in the Diocese of Las Cruces, also provides some useful reflections. Youth ministry leaders come to know the stages of human development through the study of theories from psychologists such as Abraham Maslow and Erik Erikson. According to these experts, adolescents are in the stage of life where they are discovering their identity. They are immersed in specific generational markers, which distinguish them from the previous generation, typically called *youth culture*.

Ms. Cassetta says the error in this formation is presenting adolescent development and youth culture as a homogeneous reality. Using the culture metaphor of the iceberg, youth culture is the visible tip of the iceberg, while the hidden majority of the iceberg is the culture of origin, which heavily influences how young people experience youth. Young people around the world may like similar music, dress, and even food. However, their values and their identity are developed and deeply rooted in their culture of origin. Youth Ministry was slow to recognize this difference and to respond accordingly. This way of thinking has given direction to leaders of Latino youth and young adult ministry in designing programs specifically geared to them.

Dr. Ken Johnson-Mondragón shares invaluable data on how to minister to young people and young adults. He presents the pastoral needs of Latino youth according to the four categories mentioned earlier.

Young Latinos have strong spiritual needs. *Immigrant workers* need faith-based communities grounded in their culture of origin. *Identity seekers* require mentoring to integrate their faith and their lives amid cultural transition. *Mainstream movers* need guidance to overcome the pitfalls of individualism and consumerism, and to value their Latino spiritual background. *Gang members and high-risk youth* need to develop their faith, experience healing, and move from anger to forgiveness.

To develop intellectually, immigrant workers need accessible alternative systems of education. Identity seekers need encouragement to finish high school and guidance to pursue higher education. Mainstream movers need help to find financial aid for higher education. Gang members and high-risk youth need alternative systems of education.

To achieve effective maturity and socialization, immigrant workers require a healthy environment in which to develop personal relationships. Identity seekers need to develop self-esteem and faith in themselves. Mainstream movers need to experience role models of social and cultural integration. Gang members and high-risk youth need peer groups along with a healthy place in which to belong as well as positive role models.

To acquire human virtues, immigrant workers need to avoid the pitfalls of vice and addictions. Identity seekers need guidance and direction in life. Mainstream movers need to value community service and social justice. Gang members and high-risk youth require counseling to overcome bad habits and attitudes.

The Story of Father Greg Boyle, S.J.

Identifying *what* needs to be done for Latino youth is important. Equally, if not more important, is *how* to help our youth. While I am not proposing a one-size-fits-all model, one successful example is Homeboy Industries, founded by Father Greg Boyle, S.J. Homeboy Industries traces its roots back to 1988 when, in an effort to address the escalating problems and unmet needs of gang-involved youth, Fr. Greg and many community members established positive alternatives, including an elementary school, a day-care program, and finding legitimate employment for young people. In 1992, as a response to the civil unrest in Los Angeles, Fr. Greg launched the first social enterprise business: Homeboy Bakery. The mission of Homeboy's social enterprises is to create an environment that provides training, work experience, and, above all, the opportunity for rival gang members to work side by side.

Homeboy Industries' nonprofit economic development enterprises have grown to include Homeboy Silkscreen & Embroidery, Homeboy/Homegirl Merchandise, Homegirl Café & Catering, Homeboy Farmers Market, and Homeboy Diner at Los Angeles City Hall.[5] Each year, over fifteen thousand former gang members from across Los Angeles come through Homeboy Industries' doors in an effort to make a positive change.[6]

---

[5] Homeboy Industries, http://www.homeboyindustries.org/fatherg/.

[6] TEDx Talks, *Compassion and Kinship: Fr. Gregory Boyle* (2012), https://www.youtube.com/watch?v=ipR0kWt1Fkc.

What Fr. Greg discovered is that a lethal absence of hope leads kids into gangs. This model has been adopted in forty-six different programs across the country and internationally—from Alabama and Idaho to Guatemala and Scotland. Fr. Gregory Boyle has many stories of the *how* of redemption, of the soul feeling its worth.

The Future of the Church and Latino Youth

The future of Catholicism in the United States rests heavily on the ability of the church to attract and retain young Latinos. This task begins in the parish.

It is important for youth and young adults to see their priest/pastor involved in youth ministry—not just allowing the ministry but also actively participating. How wonderful to witness young people who point out their priest to one another, as the priest contributes to the faith-filled community.

My advice is that priests and other pastors should not forget the young in their preaching. Invite the youth to speak at Mass, not as a homily but perhaps at the end of Mass to give their witness, especially after they have gone to a retreat or attended an event that has brought them closer to Jesus.

The young are already part of the church. They are waiting to be invited to participate in liturgical ministry as lectors, altar servers, extraordinary Eucharistic ministers (after they have received the sacrament of Confirmation), and ushers. It is a wonderful idea to invite young people to sit on the consultative boards of the parish, that is, the parish and finance councils. Young parishioners can be welcomed to the outreach parish programs to support the needs of the poor, the sick, the elderly, the disabled, and other people in need in the community.

We must meet young people where they are in their lives. There are ways to involve all youth without excluding anyone. Especially at the initiation of our ministry to them, we must ensure that all young people feel welcomed and valued. They are at a sensitive age, and they may feel rejected by parish adults. It is sometimes necessary to spend the beginning of any program developing rapport and trust before moving on to deeper subjects.

Communications technology to reach youth and young adults should be current and relevant and something familiar to them. I offer my own experience as an example. At a gathering with young people, we handed out flyers for a retreat, and one of the young men told us, "We don't look at things like flyers, we use this," and he handed me his smartphone.

Peers are the greatest influence, but when young people need guidance, they turn to their parents. As much as possible, parents should be involved in the faith and human development of their adolescent and young adult children. Youth ministries with parental support and encouragement offer incredible potential to provide guidance for the transition from adolescence to adulthood. In parishes in our diocese, we offer opportunities for the parents and young people to attend meetings and events together. One example is the preparation for the sacrament of Confirmation. Embracing parents and working together to support young people sometimes has the added benefit of bringing the parents back to the faith.

The parish cannot ignore the need to provide programs for youth and young adults in addition to Confirmation, and it would be wise to invest money and other resources in youth evangelization. The US bishops encourage advocacy, catechesis, community life, evangelization, justice and service, leadership development, pastoral care, and prayer and worship.

When a parish gets serious about retention of young people, it is time to hire people on a full-time basis to create and implement creative programs. When an individual parish cannot afford this, it may be necessary for more than one parish to share resources and hire youth ecclesial ministers who will provide youth ministry for more than one parish. This is the case for two parishes in our diocese. The two parishes successfully combined their Religious Education programs. There are 75 volunteer catechists and 1,200 children enrolled in the program.

Last but most significant is budgeting. Parishes need to provide financial backing for a youth minister. Other funding needs include youth and adult volunteer support, retreats, catechetical formation, leadership programs, youth evangelization, prayer and worship, mission trips, and pastoral care needs.

I realize budgets are not always a popular topic. However, the church recognizes the importance of keeping young people in the Catholic faith. Youth ministry is one way to make that happen, and that takes dedicated human and financial resources.

To provide funds for youth and young adult ministries could be a line item in parish and diocesan annual budgets. If a parish provides youth ministry for adolescents, young adult ministry should follow. Fund-raising can provide annual income support for programs. If your parish belongs to a mission diocese, like ours, grant funding may help to support youth and young adult ministries.

Looking at the future, the church must provide funds in the budget for youth and young adult ministries. In order to retain young Catholics, the church needs to reach out to high school students and young adults in ways that interest and maintain a strong connection between young people and the church.

Latino Youth as Missionary Disciples

The Second Vatican Council teaches us that the call to holiness is universal, and this call includes young people. Young people must be challenged not to be afraid to encounter Jesus Christ. Pope Benedict XVI addressed young people in his homily during the Mass for inauguration of the Pontificate on Sunday, April 24, 2005, in St. Peter's Square:

> And so, today, with great strength and great conviction, on the basis of long personal experience of life, I say to you, dear young people: Do not be afraid of Christ! He takes nothing away, and he gives you everything. When we give ourselves to him, we receive a hundredfold in return. Yes, open, open wide the doors to Christ—and you will find true life. Amen.

Pope Francis has a genuine love for young people. In Paraguay in July 2015, Pope Francis said to the youth, "Make a mess, but then also help to tidy it up." His Holiness went on to say, "A mess which gives us a free heart, a mess which gives us solidarity, a mess which gives us hope."

In conclusion, Pope Francis told the young people, "We don't want young weaklings. We do not want young people who tire quickly, who live life worn out with faces of boredom. We want youths with hope and strength."

Young people are each other's best evangelizers. What is true of everyone is true of young people: most of us do not meet Jesus in direct and personal revelation, but rather through others. It is notably true among teenagers that they want to emulate their peers and not necessarily the adult people in their lives. Young people experience being missionary disciples when they are faithful disciples of Jesus among their peers.

What is infectious is the joy frequently found among young people, and there is nothing more joyful than the experience of Jesus in real and palpable ways.

Chapter 5

Privilege and Responsibility of Citizenship

It was when I began to teach as part of the team at the Mexican–American Cultural Center (MACC) in San Antonio, Texas, that social and political matters became an incredibly deep part of me. In my youth, I became aware of the racial and cultural biases around me, and for a long time my thinking was, "Well, that's just the way it is." I learned to accept our Mexican–American underclass.

Nevertheless, the ideas of fairness, justice, and equality were innate in me, things that were intuitive to my heart. I recall the first time I heard of a strike by workers. My mother, María, and my Aunt Tomasa worked with a good number of other Mexican–American women and a few men at the People's Laundry. Their wages were very low, and it was before minimum wages were standard, at least in Bay City. The workers at the laundry organized a strike. I remember my mother and aunt expressing their satisfaction when they heard their boss was having a hard time getting other people to work at his People's Laundry. The strike was a success, and the workers received the raise they wanted.

In high school, we seniors had to write a term paper, a task we all dreaded but that became one of the best things to prepare me for university. We had to choose a theme, and I wanted to write on the

history and the plight of Mexican–Americans. The library had nothing
that would help me do the research, so I had to give up on the idea.
There was a good deal on the history and plight of African Americans,
and that became my second choice. The research I did was enlightening,
and I could relate much of my Mexican–American background to the
experience of African Americans. That work left in my young heart a
profound regard for all people who suffer racism and injustice.

*   *   *

The ten years I spent in Mexico as a seminarian and later
as a missionary priest exposed me to the terrible conditions of
those in the Third World as well as to the absence of certain
human and civil rights. The strict laws rooted in the Mexican
Constitution of 1918, which outlawed much of the church's
work, such as education and ownership of property, prohib-
ited the work of foreign priests and missionaries. Clerical garb
and religious habits were outlawed. The church in Mexico
had ways of doing its work in spite of these restrictions, but it
all had to be done discreetly. We foreign missionaries had to
keep a low profile so as not to suffer deportation. We had to
stay away from social and political involvement, and not get
involved in such things as protests and social movements.

When I returned to the United States in 1976 to work at
MACC in San Antonio, it was exciting to see Latino activism
so alive. Among the prominent figures in politics were US
Representative Henry B. Gonzàles and Mayor Henry Cisne-
ros, who later became the Secretary of Housing and Urban
Development.

Citizens Organized for Public Service (COPS), a community organization founded by the Industrial Areas Foundation (IAF) and organized by Ernesto Cortez, drove the Latino
population's involvement in San Antonio. Saul Alinsky, a social

theorist who was introduced to the Archbishop of Milan (later Pope Paul VI) by Jacques Maritain, a Thomistic philosopher who served as a consultant on some of the Second Vatican Council proceedings, founded the IAF.

The Archdiocese of San Antonio encouraged its parishes, particularly those on the west side where the population was heavily Mexican–American, to be part of COPS. William (known as Willie) Velásquez used San Antonio as the base for the Southwest Voter Registration Education Project; I expand his story below.

MACC itself was seeing its best years. Father Virgilio Elizondo, an archdiocesan priest who saw a need for preparing people for ministry among Latinos in the United States, founded MACC. He presented the idea and gained support from the Texas Catholic Conference of Bishops, and from PADRES, a national organization of Latino priests. It helped that Bishop Patricio Flores had become the first Latino bishop as Auxiliary Bishop of San Antonio the year before the founding of MACC. Enthusiastic support also came from Archbishop Francis Furey, who made buildings and housing available on the campus of Assumption Seminary.

MACC had a language and cultural thrust, but it was also heavy on social justice. Fr. Elizondo connected with other pastoral institutes such as the Institut Catolique of Paris, the East Asian Pastoral Institute in Manila, the Instituto Pastoral de Latino América, and the National Office of Catechesis in Mexico City. He later became friends with Latin American and other theologians such as Fr. Gustavo Gutiérrez of Peru; Fr. Oscar Beozzo of Brazil; Fr. Jose Marins, also of Brazil; Fr. Johannes Hofinger, SJ, from Manila; Fr. John Linskens of Belgium; and Dr. Enrique Dussel from Argentina. These theologians lectured at MACC and brought the influence of Latin American theology to Latino church leaders in the United States.

My experiences in Mexico as a missionary and at MACC as a teacher and participant prepared me well to become a bishop. Further, both experiences convinced me of the words of the Second Vatican Council in *Gaudium et Spes*, "The joy and hope, the grief and anguish of the people of our time, especially of those who are poor or afflicted in any way, are the joy and hope, the grief and anguish of the followers of Christ as well."

Latino Activism

The diocese of which I am the bishop emeritus is at the frontier, which means that it is far from centers of power, influence, and control. Things look different from the frontier. Perhaps that is why prophets emerge from the frontier, including Jesus himself, who came from Galilee, far from the centers of power in Jerusalem and Rome. From the vantage point of the frontier, we may recognize the flaws in what is going on in the great centers of learning and authority. In the category of frontier, I would also place minorities, or people on the edge, those who are marginalized, and who at times recognize that the status quo is not in keeping with the highest ideals of human wholeness or consistent with the dignity and respect demanded by human personhood. In this way, they function as prophets. These people help create a better world when they claim their own human and civil rights.

The African American people, under the leadership of Dr. Martin Luther King Jr., helped awaken Latinos to the reality of racial bias and discrimination they, too, endured. The farmworker movement, led by César Chávez, inspired in Latinos a greater appreciation for civil rights. César Chávez alerted us to the inhuman condition of farmworkers.

"César Estrada Chávez," Senator Robert F. Kennedy noted, was "one of the heroic figures of our time." He was a devout Catholic who did not simply believe the teachings of Jesus Christ; he was transformed by them. They guided his efforts to secure just treatment for migrant workers. He taught the social teachings of Pope Leo XIII to farmworkers at strike rallies. He did not simply form unions. He established tight-knit community organizations. He gathered the Mexican–Americans in Delano, California, formed the United Farm Workers, and led a strike against local table grape growers. The struggle for just contracts was long and drawn out. Rejecting violence at all times, he resorted to fasting and doing penance to draw national attention to the blatantly unjust wages and working and living conditions of the Hispanic migrant laborers in California. He was not only one of the great labor leaders of the century; he was also a heroic example of Catholic moral leadership. Two weeks before he died, he visited us at the Pastoral Center of the Diocese of Las Cruces.

Throughout the country, there are stories of individuals and groups that contributed to the involvement of Latinos in the democratic process. Every major city (e.g., Chicago, New York, Newark, Houston, Santa Fe, Denver, Miami, and Los Angeles) provides an example where Latino leaders have emerged and found success in the election of Latino legislators and other leaders in local, state, and federal government. I am most familiar with San Antonio, Texas, and New Mexico, mainly because I witnessed events there firsthand and saw the effects of those efforts. What I have seen has been not only educational but also inspiring to me personally.

Before World War II, only New Mexico could claim any tradition of Latinos holding federal elected office. The first Latino US senator, O. A. Larrazolo, was elected in 1929. The first Latino to serve in the House of Representatives, Benigno

(B. C.) Hernández, served from 1915 to 1916 and from 1919 to 1920. Other Latinos to serve in that position were Nestor Montoya, 1921 to 1922, and Dennis Chávez, who served in the House of Representatives from 1931 to 1935 and the US Senate from 1935 to 1962.[1]

A major breakthrough for Latinos in political life came with the election of John F. Kennedy. His candidacy in 1960 involved both Henry B. González and Edward Roybal, both World War II veterans. In forming Viva Kennedy clubs in the Southwest, Latinos helped Kennedy win in states like Texas and New Mexico, where Kennedy won 70 percent of the Latino vote. Nationwide, he won 85 percent of the Latino vote.[2]

Henry B. González of San Antonio and Edward Roybal of Los Angeles were the first Latino council members in their respective cities since the mid-twentieth century—Roybal in 1949 and Gonzalez in 1953. Both were later elected to the US House of Representatives, where González served from 1962 to 1999, and Roybal seved from 1963 to 1975. Eligio (known as Kika) de la Garza from Texas became a US representative in 1965, and Joseph Montoya became a US senator in 1964.

New organizations among Latinos were active from the mid-1960s to the mid-1970s. Juan Gonzalez describes them this way: "The brash new groups—the Brown Berets, La Raza Unida, the Alianza, the United Farm Workers, the Young Lords, Los Siete de la Raza, the Crusade for Justice, Movimiento Pro Independencia, MECHA, the August Twenty-Ninth Movement—were invariably younger and usually from lower-class origins than the established civic organizations."[3] Not as radical were the United Farm Workers and the National Council

---

[1] Juan Gonzalez, *Harvest of Empire: A History of Latinos in America* (New York: Penguin Books, rev. ed. 2011), 170–71.

[2] Ibid., 171.

[3] Ibid., 174.

of La Raza (NCLR). From the NCLR emerged the Mexican–American Legal Defense and Education Fund (MALDEF) and the Southwest Voter Registration Education Project (SVREP).[4]

Willie Velásquez founded the SVREP in 1974. Before this, he had founded the Mexican–American Youth Organization, as a young community organizer for the Catholic Bishops' Committee for the Spanish-Speaking, the precursor to the Office of Hispanic Affairs of the United States Conference of Catholic Bishops (USCCB). Together with the Mexican–American Legal Defense Fund (MALDEF), the SVREP helped restructure the political scene in the Southwest, at city, county, district, and state levels, by changing at-large elections to single-member districts.[5]

Thanks to Velásquez's work and that of others, hundreds of minority people have been elected to public offices throughout the Southwest. Over two and a half million people are registered to vote, and they are making a marked impact in local, state, and national elections. Much of what he did was by means of using the judicial system, knowing the law and applying it to situations where injustice existed. In 1995, President Bill Clinton awarded Velásquez the Presidential Medal of Freedom, the highest honor any civilian can receive; he was one of the first Latinos to win the prestigious honor.

Some extraordinarily important events took place in the state of New Mexico, which contributed to the political enfranchisement of Latinos at the state and nationwide levels. Frank I. Sánchez, of Roswell, New Mexico, learned the importance and impact of grassroots organizing from his father, who was a labor organizer and construction worker. Under Frank Sánchez's leadership, the Chicano Youth Associa-

---

[4] Ibid., 171–72.
[5] Ibid., 177.

tion (CYA) was founded; chapters of the CYA were organized across southern New Mexico. The CYA led efforts for educational reforms. The landmark case, *Serna v. Portales Municipal Schools* (1972) set a national precedent for the institutionalization of bilingual education.

Sanchez founded several organizations to address labor, health, and political issues affecting Mexican–Americans, including the Southern New Mexico Legal Services (SNMLS) in 1976. Through the SNMLS, he worked against the state's system of gerrymandering and eventually was responsible for the lawsuit, *Sánchez v. King* (1982), based on the Voting Rights Act, which successfully contended that the legislative redistricting plan violated the voting rights of Mexican–Americans and Native Americans in New Mexico. This also set a national precedent for the inclusion of Latinos and other minorities in the democratic process.

Latino Voting Trends

When I use the broad-based term *Latino*, there are of course commonalities as well as differences within the Latino cultures. Latinos represent a mixture of immigrant and native born, differing income and educational levels, both Spanish-language dominant and English-language dominant. Latinos originate from the Caribbean, Mexico, Central and South America, and their immigration patterns into the United States have taken various routes. They share a worldview around family, identity, time, spirituality, and relationships, yet there are differences in educational levels, language skills, income levels, and cultural values.

In the United States today, Latinos number more than fifty million, and more are registering to vote. Antonio González, of the William C. Velásquez Institute, says, "Politically, the biggest single unifier among subgroups across the Latino community is compatibility on issues." According to several Pew Research Center studies, the number of Latino eligible voters has reached more than 25 million in 2014, up from 17.3 million in 2006. Historically, Latino voter turnout rates are among the lowest of any race or ethnic group in midterm elections. In 2010, 31.2 percent of Latinos voted, compared with 48.6 percent of whites, 44 percent of blacks, and 31 percent of Asians. Some eight hundred thousand Latinos—the vast majority US born—turn eighteen each year, a demographic wave projected to double the Latino electorate by 2030.

Latinos are less likely to be registered to vote than white or black Americans. According to 2013 data from Gallup, only 51 percent of all eligible Latino residents were registered to vote in the 2012 federal elections. At the same time, 85 percent of white voters, 60 percent of Asian voters, and 81 percent of black voters were registered.

Many Latinos are not American-born citizens, which explains, in part, the low voter registration numbers. The number of Latinos who registered to vote in 2012 reached 13.7 million, up 18 percent over 2008, which was also a record. However, the voter turnout rate among Latino registered voters was lower in 2012 than in 2008—81.7 percent versus 84 percent. Participation increases with citizenship status, generation, income, and education. According to the Latino National Survey,[6] in answer to the question as to how interested Latinos are in politics and public affairs, a considerable portion responded "not interested," and the most common response among the first generation (citizens and noncitizens) and the second generation is at least "somewhat interested." Higher

---

[6] Luis R. Fraga, John A. Garcia, and Rodney E. Hero, *Latinos in the New Millennium: An Almanac of Opinion, Behavior, and Policy Preferences* (New York: Cambridge University Press, 2011).

economic status among Latinos considerably increases the degree of interest.

The survey examined the sense of trust in government. It indicates strong reservations about government's concern for the common good, its trustworthiness, and one's ability to influence or understand government. Large majorities believe government is "run by just a few big interests looking out for themselves and not the benefit of all." This view increases from the first to the second generation. Higher levels of education and income spur a stronger sense of government being mostly run by "just a few big interests."[7]

Many non-American-born citizens come from countries beset by corruption, lack of transparency and lack of rule of law, and patterns of impunity, and without respectable judicial systems. Some may be influenced by periods of military and other dictatorships where there was no semblance of democracy or respect for civil and human rights. Although we in this country have had a democratic system in place for over two hundred years, democracy is relatively new throughout Latin America.

Roughly 60 percent of Latinos identify themselves as Democrats. Because Mexican–Americans dominate the national pan-Latino community through sheer numbers—they make up about 60 percent of the total Latino population—and they are concentrated in key electoral states like Texas and California, simple arithmetic and political logic make it likely that one of the next national political leaders will be a Mexican–American Democrat.

The future of this country will be even more representative of Latinos, and the present statistics reveal this. One in five of those in the United States are Latino, one in four children from kindergarten to twelfth grade are Latino, and one-third of the American Catholic Church is Latino.

---

[7] Ibid.

To engage Latinos in the democratic process, there must be an element of trust and respect in their relationship with their leaders. Greater acceptance comes when Latino leaders are involved in the community. Among the common traits among all Latino cultures, exhibiting respect is critical. As President of Mexico, Benito Juárez stated, "El respeto al derecho ajeno es la paz" (Respect for the rights of others leads to peace).

Church Teaching on Civic Responsibility

The Catechism of the Catholic Church (CCC) brings together sources of the church's teaching on civic responsibility such as the teachings of the Second Vatican Council, specifically *Gaudium et Spes*; papal encyclicals such as St. John XXIII's *Pacem in Terris;* and *Mater et Magistra*. The CCC teaches there is a certain resemblance between unity of the divine persons in God and the fraternity that we ought to establish among ourselves. The CCC further states the human being needs life in society to develop in accordance with human nature. The CCC states the human being is and ought to be the principle, the subject, and the object of every social organization.

The CCC develops the concept of the common good, which is defined as "the sum total of social conditions which allow people, either as groups or as individuals, to reach their fulfillment more fully and more easily" (CCC no. 1906). It concerns the life of all and calls for prudence from each, principally from those who exercise authority. Common good consists of three essential elements: First, respect for the human being and human rights, freedom to pursue the human vocation, and freedom of religion. Second, it requires the social well-being and development of the group itself. Authority is to make accessible to each what is needed to lead a truly human life: food, clothing, health, work, education and culture, suitable information, and the right to establish a family. The third requirement is that of peace, that is, the stability and security of a just order. It is the basis of the right to legitimate personal and collective defense.

The CCC calls for participation in public life—a voluntary and generous engagement of a person in social interchange. It is necessary that all participate, each according to his position and role, in promoting the common good. This obligation is inherent in the dignity of the human being. Those who exercise authority are to inspire the confidence of the members of the group and encourage them to put themselves at the service of others. Quoting *Gaudium et Spes*, the CCC teaches, "The future of humanity is in the hands of those who are capable of providing the generations to come with reasons for life and optimism" (*Gaudium et Spes*, no. 31).

In his speech to Congress on September 24, 2015, Pope Francis spoke about the important vocation of elected officials. He said that their responsibility as members of Congress is to enable this country, by its legislative activity, to grow as a nation. He reminded them that they are the face of its people, their representatives, and that they are called to defend and preserve the dignity of their fellow citizens, "in the tireless and demanding pursuit of the common good, for this is the chief aim of all politics."

Pope Francis also reminded Congress that all political activity must serve and promote the good of the human being based on respect for his or her dignity. He said that if politics is truly at the service of the human being, it cannot be a slave to the economy and finance. "Politics is, instead, an expression of our compelling need to live as one, in order to build as one of the greatest common good: that of a community which sacrifices particular interests in order to share, in justice and peace, its goods, its interests, its social life."

The USCCB publishes "Forming Consciences for Faithful Citizenship" a year before every general election. Published in both English and Spanish, the document provides a framework for Catholics in the United States. It is a teaching document on the political responsibility of Catholics, updated and reissued by the full body of bishops at its general meeting.[8]

It does not offer a voter's guide, scorecard of issues, or direction on how to vote. It applies Catholic moral principles to a range of important issues and warns against misguided appeals to conscience to ignore fundamental moral claims, to reduce Catholic moral concerns to one or two matters, or to justify choices simply to advance partisan, ideological, or personal interests.

In the second part of "Forming Consciences for Faithful Citizenship," the bishops include Catholic teaching on major issues that they are to consider when deciding how to vote. These issues include the right to life and the dignity of the human being; the call to family, community, and participation; rights and responsibilities; option for the poor and vulnerable; dignity of work and rights of workers; immigration; solidarity; and care for God's creation. The document provides a summary of policy positions of the USCCB. The bishops call attention to issues with significant moral dimensions that should be carefully considered in each campaign and as policy decisions are made in the years to come. Some issues involve principles that can never be violated, such as the fundamental right to life.

---

[8] "Forming Consciences for Faithful Citizenship" (November 2015), http://www.usccb.org/issues-and-action/faithful-citizenship/upload/forming-consciences-for-faithful-citizenship.pdf.

What Needs to Be Done

The duty of the church, especially its leaders, is to educate people about their civic responsibility. We have seen how Latinos could participate more in our democratic system. We need to educate both those who are born citizens and those who become citizens about not only their rights and privileges as citizens but also about their responsibilities, which include engagement in public life.

It is exceedingly important that we, in our teaching and preaching, connect the teachings of Jesus Christ with our lives in society. So much of what Jesus teaches is about right relationships among people. Our teaching should aim to form consciences in order that disciples of Christ make political decisions according to Christian principles.

In teaching concern for the common good and social justice, we are to keep in mind the need to include everyone. Participation in civic matters is important for those who are concerned for themselves and for their children with a view not only to the present but also to the future. Decisions are made, at the local and national levels, by legislators and other authorities that affect our day-to-day lives. That is why it is important to educate ourselves on issues that will benefit everyone. Our aim is for everything that is good, fair, and right. Parishes must promote voter registration and encourage participation at all elections at the local and national levels. Parishes also should encourage those who register to exercise their responsibility to vote. This encouragement is exceptionally opportune before all elections.

Our Latino families ought to be concerned about who represents them on school boards, city councils, county commissions, and state and national offices. We must be attentive to recognizing potential leadership among our Latinos, in particular those who have the talent, education, intelligence, and passion for the common good.

Our Latino people are to be encouraged to join organizations that are not only political but also those that promote the good of all, such as community organizations, veterans' groups, neighborhood groups, labor unions, parent–teacher associations, and Latino organizations (e.g., GI Forum, the National Council of La Raza, and the League of United Latin American Citizens).

While still in his forties, Willie Velásquez became a cancer victim; his passing came quickly. The night that Willie died, he told his wife and the few friends that were present at his deathbed that he was extremely tired, and he probably would not make it through the night. Later that night, he woke for the last time, held his wife's hand, and said, "¡Qué bonito es el nuevo mundo!" which means, "How beautiful the new world is!" Then, he repeated, "¡Qué bonito es el nuevo mundo!" and died.

What Willie Velásquez meant by that phrase will always be open to interpretation. He could have been referring to how beautiful the vision of heaven is. He also could have been looking at the accomplishments of his life and seen how much more beautiful the world is because of what he did. It could have been the vision of the new heavens and the new earth, the Kingdom of God, articulated by Jesus himself in the Gospels—the Kingdom where peace, justice, mercy, love, and understanding reign. I suppose this is what we are all about in our pastoral and social ministry, doing our bit to make the world more beautiful, according to the plan of God, and perhaps at the end of it all, we can say with Willie, "¡Qué bonito es el nuevo mundo!"

Chapter 6

Crossing Borders—
The Moral and Legal Challenge

In my own childhood, I recall that the US Border Patrol was active in South Texas where I grew up. One man my family befriended had a good job in Bay City. He always dressed neatly and even looked professional. We admired him for his intelligent conversations, and he seemed to be knowledgeable about many things. One weekend we went to Houston, Texas, to visit relatives and to go shopping. Our friend went along, and as we were walking on the sidewalk in downtown Houston, a Border Patrol vehicle pulled up, and our friend was placed in the Border Patrol vehicle and taken to jail. We were shocked that they would pick him, and only him, from our small group as well as the fact that he was tagged as being an undocumented citizen. Later in the day, we visited him while he was in jail, and he admitted to us that he was indeed undocumented. He expected to be deported to Mexico soon. As a small child, this was my first encounter with immigration authorities, and it left me deeply sad.

For years, the bishops and priests on both sides of the border at Anapra, New Mexico, and Ciudad Juárez, Mexico, concelebrate a Mass on two altars at the border fence. In 2014, at the border Mass, Yoryet Lara, age twelve, and her ten-year-old sister Jocelyn were able to greet their mother but only with the palms of their hands pressed against

*the border fence that separated them. Their mother, Trinidad, once lived
illegally in the United States in El Paso, Texas. She was employed, paid
her bills, and never got into trouble, until she was stopped seven years
ago for running a stop sign. She was later deported.*

*As they met at the fence, the mother sobbed, "Don't cry, my
queens, don't cry. I love you all very much, my daughters."*

"Mommy, I miss you! Ay, Mommy!" said Jocelyn.[1]

*   *   *

Celebrating the border Mass in 2009, I invited all present
on both sides of the border to look toward the east, to Mount
Cristo Rey, where we find the monument to Christ the King. I
asked everyone to reflect on what Our Lord sees from that cross.

From my perspective, Christ sees the many inhumanities,
violence, and injustice. He sees all that happens along this border with sorrow and tears. What Christ sees is contrary to the
Kingdom that He came to preach and establish. We ought
to see the reality of our times, but even more, we must also
share the same vision as Jesus had when he preached about
his Kingdom.

At the Mass, I preached that all of us ought to see not only
the way things are but also the way things should be. Christ
wants us to share the vision of his Kingdom and continue to
fight for a more beautiful world so that his people may be
more joyful. Growing together in faith and hope is one way
that His Kingdom will be fulfilled here on this earth: the kingdom of justice, peace, and love.

---

[1] Bishop Ricardo Ramírez, C.S.B., "Crossing Borders: A Moral and Legal
Challenge," *Traces Magazine Online* (December 3, 2004), http://www.traceson-
line.org/2014/12/crossing-borders-a-moral-and-legal-challenge/.

The Global Situation

The full horror of the migrant tragedy in Europe was recently captured in the filming of the tragic death of a toddler found lying face down on a beach in Turkey. The young boy was one of many Syrians who drowned trying to reach Greece. A second image of a police officer carrying the young boy's body from the beach breaks our hearts and puts a face on the dire circumstances of the hundreds of thousands seeking asylum in the European Union.

This sad incident is only one example of the plight of immigrants, not just in the United States but also around the globe. In recent months, a surge of migrants from the Middle East and Africa has put pressure on European countries, especially Italy, Greece, and Hungary. Border crossings were up from 280,000 in 2014 to 350,000 in January–August of 2015. The conflicts in Syria and Afghanistan and abuses in Eritrea are major drivers of the migration, according to a recent BBC report.[2]

According to the BBC report, four million refugees have fled Syria's civil war. More than 2,600 migrants drowned in the Mediterranean during the same period. Some of the worst tragedies include the death of five hundred migrants on two boats that sank on August 27, 2015, after leaving Zuwara in Libya. We were horrified by the discovery of seventy-one bodies, believed to be Syrian migrants, on an abandoned truck in Austria on August 27, 2015; the death of an estimated eight hundred migrants off Lampedusa Island on April 19, 2015, due to a shipwreck; and the death of an estimated three hundred migrants who drowned during rough seas in February 2015.

---

[2] BBC News, "Why Is EU Struggling with Migrants and Asylum?" (September 1, 2015), http://www.bbc.com/news/world-europe-24583286.

The good news is that, as of this writing, several countries have opened their borders to receive many of these refugees, including Great Britain, Spain, France, and Austria, which joined Germany in welcoming refugees on humanitarian grounds. Jordan, Turkey, and Lebanon have been accommodating Syrian refugees for years, since these countries border Syria. Venezuela, Brazil, Argentina, and Uruguay accepted Syrian refugees as well. As of this writing, the United States has agreed to take ten thousand refugees for the coming fiscal year, and has given the most aid, $574 million, or 31 percent of all the aid given worldwide.

In 2013, the United Nations reported there were 232 million immigrants worldwide.[3] Pope Francis, in his recent address to the VII World Congress of the Pastoral Care of Migrants, referred to the pain felt by migrants when they leave their countries of origin: "We find the effects on infants and young people who grow up without one or both parents, and the risk of marriages failing due to prolonged absences."

The US Church and Immigration

The United States, we say, is a nation of immigrants, but so is the U.S. Catholic Church. The surge in immigration in the latter part of the nineteenth century started the enormous growth in the Catholic population of the United States. Americans whose families had been here since the beginning of English colonization were mainly non-Catholic, so when the new immigrants started arriving from Catholic Europe, there was a backlash against them precisely because they were Catholic. The Know-Nothing Party was especially notorious

---

[3] "The Number of International Migrants Worldwide Reaches 232 Million," *UN Population Facts* 2013/2 (September 2013), http://esa.un.org/unmigration/documents/the_number_of_international_migrants.pdf.

in its attacks against Catholics, even to the point of burning of churches and convents.

The story of Irish migration is both tragic and triumphant. It was tragic because of the circumstances, caused by the great potato famine of the 1840s. The voyage across the Atlantic was harrowing for many. Charles R. Morris describes the Irish immigration in his book *American Catholic: The Saints and Sinners Who Built America's Most Powerful Church*.[4] He writes,

> Families, crowded by the hundreds into dark holes without bedding or sanitary facilities, were refused access to the decks during voyages that could stretch to six or eight weeks, survived on spoiled food and fouled water, and when the ship was tossed in ocean storms, shrieked in the darkness and rolled helplessly in filth and excrement.[5]

When they arrived in North America, they faced terrible working conditions and meager pay. They lived in filthy tenements and were objects of scorn by non-Catholics. The triumphant side is that some Irish people were successful economically and socially. In the Catholic Church, Irish clergy became most prominent, including many bishops and cardinals.

Other groups were the Italians and Eastern Europeans. These people, too, suffered from blatant discrimination and disdain from established citizens. It was during this time in the nineteenth century that the Catholic parochial school system began. The parochial schools were established mainly because Catholic children suffered heavy persecution. As Archbishop Dennis Joseph Dougherty said, "A parochial school is a neces-

---

[4] Charles R. Morris, *American Catholic: The Saints and Sinners Who Built America's Most Powerful Church* (New York: Random House, 1977).

[5] Ibid., 36.

sity, especially in this country where our children breathe in an atmosphere of heresy, unbelief and sometimes irreligion. By many, the Catholic Church is here ridiculed, scoffed at, despised and persecuted; not by sword, but by hatred and opposition."[6] The American bishops made it obligatory for Catholic children to attend parochial schools.

Latino Immigration in History

The ancestors of Latinos were in what is now the United States since the settlement of Spaniards and Mexicans in northern New Mexico in the early seventeenth century. The people of Puerto Rico became US citizens when the United States took over the island in 1898. The history of the influx of Mexican immigrants is noteworthy after 1910 for various reasons. First of all, 1910 marked the beginning of the Mexican Revolution (a civil war), which lasted about ten years, during which time people fled to the north because of the turmoil in their country as well as unemployment. It was during that time that my own family migrated from San Luis Potosí in 1914, when my mother was barely one year old. On the US side, work on the railroads, as well as farmwork, attracted immigrants, particularly when the US became engaged in World War I, and laborers became scarce. This was when US law made it illegal for Asians to migrate into the country.

Many from Mexico fled persecution during the aftermath of the Mexican Revolution. During this time, the church was outlawed; its priests, bishops, and religious were expelled; and churches remained closed. Violence erupted with the Cristero rebellion in the 1920s, and many died in defense of their Catholic faith.

---

[6] Quoted in ibid., 177.

The apprehension of undocumented immigrants, particularly those of Mexican descent, has been going on for a long time. During the Great Depression around 500,000 to 1 million Mexican immigrants and Mexican–Americans were deported; this removal was called *repatriation*. During that time, immigrants would be apprehended in public places, and often, without formal proceedings, were sent to Mexico. About 60 percent of those who were either deported or left on their own were American citizens. Many families lost most of their possessions, and some family members died trying to return. Certain neighborhoods in cities like Houston, San Antonio, and Los Angeles were virtually emptied.[7]

In 1942, the US government initiated the Bracero program, which allowed laborers to enter legally for short periods, but then they had to return to Mexico. Terrible injustices were committed toward the Braceros, so it was not a total success. Over four million laborers entered the United States during the Bracero program's twenty-two-year history. The program ended in 1964 amid pressure from labor unions and religious groups.

The Immigration Reform and Control Act of 1986 documented 2.7 million immigrants. It was supposed to curtail illegal immigration, especially given the strict employer sanctions that were part of the law. However, in 1986, there were an estimated five million undocumented immigrants living in the United States; by 2001, the number was estimated at eleven million. Lawmakers seriously underestimated US employers' demand for foreign workers. Through the Diocese of Las Cruces, approximately six thousand people were provided with immigration services during this time and in the

---

[7] Francisco E. Balderrama and Raymond Rodríquez, *Decade of Betrayal: Mexican Repatriation in the 1930s* (Albuquerque: University of New Mexico Press, 2006).

years following. Dioceses across the nation were involved in this process, assisted by Catholic Legal Immigration Network, Inc. (CLINIC).

The immigrant population in the United States hit a record high of 42.1 million in the second quarter of 2015, according to an analysis of monthly Census Bureau data by the Center for Immigration Studies, released on August 13, 2015. The number of immigrants rose by 1.7 million since the same time the previous year. Immigrants currently comprise 13.3 percent of the nation's total population, reaching the highest level in the nation in 105 years.

Immigration is a heated issue. While much of the discussion surrounds immigrants from Mexico, migration to the United States from its southern neighbor dropped 17.7 percent from 2010 to 2013, an average of 140,266 a year, according to the US Department of Homeland Security. These numbers show a changing picture in terms of who is coming, as well as the places they choose to settle.

Perhaps due to Mexico's stronger economy and lower birthrates, Mexicans are no longer as dominant in the ranks of new immigrants as in the last decade, though Mexico is still the single largest place of origin for new immigrants.

In the summer of 2014, 60,000 accompanied and unaccompanied children came to the US border, mainly from Central America—particularly Guatemala, Honduras, and El Salvador. There are several reasons why these children and their families desired to leave their homelands. Currently these countries are experiencing widespread violence perpetrated by gangs and drug cartels. Children are forced to participate in drug trafficking and other crimes. These countries are also experiencing a lack of economic and educational opportunities for young people.

The Border Patrol apprehended children arriving at our borders, and if they had relatives in the United States, they got temporary legal passage into the country. This is where the church came in. Parishes all along the border on the US side welcomed these children, and sometimes their mothers, provided them with showers, warm meals, clothing, and the means to contact their relatives in the United States. Their relatives would in turn send them money or tickets to travel to join them. The local parishes received donations of food, clothing, and money to assist these refugees. In most places, the response was most generous.

Sister Blandina, Child Immigrant

We can never invest too much in children, including immigrant children. I cite the story of Sister Blandina Segale, a Sister of Charity of Cincinnati. In 1854, when she was four years old, she arrived in the United States from the Piedmont area of Italy. The family crossed the Atlantic, went around Florida, entered the Mississippi River at New Orleans, and finally settled in the city of Cincinnati on the banks of the Ohio River. Sister Blandina and her blood sister, Faustina, joined the Sisters of Charity, a community dedicated especially to poor Italian immigrants and others. When assigned as a young nun to Trinidad, she thought she was going to the island of Trinidad, off the coast of Venezuela, where, she thought, she would work as a missionary with people of African descent. She found out later that she was actually being sent to Trinidad, Colorado, to work with Mexicans, Indians, cowboys, and farmers. Sister Blandina was multitalented and went to work building the first schools and hospitals in southern Colorado and northern New Mexico. Over one hundred years later, her legacy continues. Thousands of poor children receive early childhood service by her continuing ministry. The cause for Sister Blandina's beatification has been officially submitted to the Vatican. I am privileged to be the postulator for her cause.

Sister Blandina is an example of what child immigrants can become and what they can contribute to our country. Indeed, we can never invest enough in our children, whether they are born here or elsewhere. To deny them health care, education, and security will be something our society will have to pay for in the future.

The Latino Immigrant

The typical immigrant who enters the United States from its southern border is usually Latin American, mostly from Mexico and Central America. Immigrants are special people. Those who migrate are courageous, intelligent, and willing to sacrifice the comfort of their homeland, their native language, and human support system; and they uproot themselves in search of a better life for themselves and their children. They are highly motivated; their family bonds and work ethic are exceptionally strong.

In his book *The Right to Stay Home: How US Policy Drives Mexican Immigration*, David Bacon cites the many US policies and corporate activities that drive much of the migration from Mexico.[8] The North American Free Trade Agreement allows subsidized corn and other farm products from the United States to be imported into Mexico and sold for much lower prices than Mexican corn.[9] This drives Mexican farmers out of business, and many of them migrate to the United States. The same is true about apples from the state of Chihuahua. Apples are imported into Mexico from the United States, driving

---

[8] David Bacon, *The Right to Stay Home: How US Policy Drives Mexican Migration* (Boston: Beacon Press, 2013).

[9] Ibid.

the price down and making it unprofitable for Mexican apple farmers. Many of these apple farmworkers migrate to the state of Washington to work in the apple orchards, the source of the apples that drove them out of business. Meanwhile the apple farmers in Washington complain that apples from China are glutting the American market.

As Bacon observes, "The experiences of Veracruz migrants and farmers impacted by Perote pig farms established by US entrepreneurs show the close connection between US investment and trade deals in Mexico and the displacement and migration of its people." The surge of American pork production in Mexico has driven small pig farms out of business and polluted the groundwater. Thus, these small farmers are forced to emigrate north. "Protecting Mexico's environment, and the rights of migrants displaced by environmental and economic causes requires making the connection between trade reform, environmental protection, and immigrant and labor rights."[10]

These newcomers bring with them faith-driven values. They hope to find in churches something of what they left behind. The Catholic Church often serves as a refuge, as the newcomers encounter new, strange, and bewildering surroundings. They are generally eager to be invited to participate in the community, and they want to contribute in any way, large or small, to the community that receives them. Many are active lay leaders back home and bring their experience as evangelizers, catechists, musicians, and youth ministers.

US Bishops' Teaching on Immigration

The US bishops have been longtime and consistent advocates for immigration reform and have followed the tradition of welcoming the stranger. In 2003, the US and Mexican bishops

---

[10] Ibid., 4.

issued a joint statement, "Strangers No Longer—Together on the Journey of Hope."[11] Together we said that people have the right to find opportunities in their homeland. In other words, they have the right not to migrate. Further, we stated that people have the right to migrate to support themselves and their families, while sovereign nations have the right to control their borders. However, the church, along with other members of our democratic society, has the right to call for a change in laws, some of which violate basic principles of human dignity imbued by the Creator.

The US bishops hold that the broken US immigration system contributes to the exploitation of migrant workers in the workplace, their abuse by ruthless smugglers, and their deaths in the desert as they seek to find work to support their families.

Comprehensive immigration reform would eliminate a chaotic system and protect the basic dignity, and lives, of our brothers and sisters. It would require those who break the law to pay fines and taxes, learn English, and take their place in the long line to have a chance to become US citizens. This is not *amnesty*, which is defined as granting a benefit without anything in return. This *path to citizenship* is in the best interests of migrants, who are able to become full members of their communities, and our nation, which will continue to benefit from their contributions without sacrificing our long-held values as a nation of immigrants: freedom, fairness, and opportunity.

The support of the US bishops for immigration reform is not because the majority of immigrants at this point in our history are Catholic. The Catholic Church heeds Our Lord's

---

[11] United States Conference of Catholic Bishops, "Strangers No Longer—Together on the Journey of Hope" (January 22, 2003), http://www.usccb.org/issues-and-action/human-life-and-dignity/immigration/strangers-no-longer-together-on-the-journey-of-hope.cfm.

call, "For I was a stranger and you welcomed me" (Matt. 25:35). Welcoming the stranger means welcoming all children of God, regardless of their ethnicity, national origin, race, or religion. This is evident in all of the social-service programs of the Catholic Church, which base their outreach on *need*, not *creed*.

As a global institution, the Catholic Church believes that the most humane and effective long-term solution to irregular immigration is economic development in poorer countries. This would allow people to remain in their native countries and support their families in dignity. This is the church's answer to a border wall, which would not prevent irregular migration over the long term. The church believes that migration should ultimately be driven by choice, not necessity.

The main reason so many enter our borders illegally is that there are insufficient visas under the current system to come legally. Our system provides only 5,000 permanent visas for unskilled laborers to come to the United States, but the demand for their work is much higher; as many as 300,000 undocumented people each year are absorbed into the US workforce. In fact, an estimated 30 percent of those counted among the undocumented entered the country legally—with tourist or visitor visas—but overstayed their presence. Many of these are from Europe and other parts of the world, but most are from Mexico and Central America.

As the US bishops have argued,

> A worker program to permit foreign-born workers to enter the country safely and legally would help reduce illegal immigration and the loss of life in the American desert. Any program should include workplace protections, living wage levels, safeguards against the displacement of US workers, and family unity. It currently takes

years for family members to be reunited through the family-based legal immigration system. This leads to family breakdown and, in some cases, illegal immigration. Changes in family-based immigration should be made to increase the number of family visas available and reduce family reunification waiting times.[12]

The fact that the majority of immigrants are Catholic makes it more real and gives a face to the immigration question for many Catholics. Many immigrants are present in our service programs, health care centers, schools, and parishes. They benefit from Catholic Charities, the St. Vincent de Paul Society, and immigration legalization and citizenship services. The largest department at the United States Conference of Catholic Bishops is Migration and Refugee Services, which, together with CLINIC, work indefatigably processing thousands of migrants and refugees toward legalization. The mission of CLINIC is to enhance and expand delivery of legal services to indigent and low-income immigrants principally through diocesan programs. Its network comprises over 196 diocesan and other programs, with 290 field offices in 47 states. The network employs about 1,200 immigration attorneys and accredited paralegals who serve roughly 600,000 low-income immigrants each year.

We, as a Catholic community, directly witness the human consequences of a broken system each day, when immigrant families come to pastors and lay ministers for help for someone who has been detained or deported. The best way to genuinely help these families, and keep them together, is to change our immigration laws.

---

[12] United States Conference of Catholic Bishops, "Catholic Church's Position on Immigration Reform" (August 2013). http://www.usccb.org/issues-and-action/human-life-and-dignity/immigration/churchteachingonimmigrationreform.cfm.

The US bishops do not support *open borders*, but rather generous and reasonable immigration policies that serve the common good. From 1848 to 1904, the border was wide open. The traffic then was southbound, caused by great violence after the US conquest of the Hispanics in the Mexican–American War. Enforcement began in 1904 to keep the Chinese from entering. No more than seventy-five agents worked along the border then. The Border Patrol was established in 1924 with a $1 million budget. Presently the US spends $18 billion in immigration enforcement, the largest federal law enforcement budget, greater than the Federal Bureau of Investigation; the Secret Service; or the Department of Alcohol, Tobacco, and Firearms.

How do the bishops respond to the allegation that illegal immigration is heavily straining our government and social services? There are several myths in this area. First, most studies show that, although at an early age immigrants consume more than they contribute, over a lifetime, they are net contributors to our economy through the taxes they pay, the goods they produce and consume, and their labor. Moreover, legal immigrants do not qualify for welfare or health care for the first five years of their residency in the United States, while undocumented immigrants never qualify for such benefits. In fact, undocumented immigrants pay billions in income taxes each year and at least $7 billion in Social Security taxes, helping to sustain Social Security for the baby-boomer generation.

The comprehensive immigration reform that we advocate would not only provide the undocumented legal status, but also the United States would receive even more income taxes and Social Security payments from immigrants, since they would be required to register with the government and pay their full share.

Making changes to the legal immigration system would help ease pressure on our border by taking undocumented immigrants out of the enforcement equation, freeing up law enforcement to focus on those who are here to harm us—drug smugglers, human traffickers, and would-be terrorists—and not those simply looking for a job.

Migration and Hospitality in Sacred Scripture

Jesus shows the way, leads the way to the awesome border—the frontier—of the new Kingdom. He invites his disciples to "come and see" (John 1:39). Jesus the migrant moved physically from place to place. With Mary and Joseph, he went from Bethlehem to Egypt, and then traveled with his family to Galilee. In the Gospel of Luke, his entire ministry was a journey from Galilee to Jerusalem, the destined place of his death and resurrection.

Theologically, we can say that God crosses borders: between divinity and humanity.[13] Making our earth his dwelling place in the person of Jesus, God leads us from the old law to the new law of the spirit, from the covenant with the people of Israel to believers everywhere, from the male-dominant and patriarchal societal and religious customs of the day to the inclusion of women—even in leadership positions in his ministry. He transfers his ministry from his own culture, the world of the Jews, to include the Samaritans and the Gentiles, and thus makes his saving plan to include everyone and exclude no one. "I was a stranger and you welcomed me" (Matt. 25:35).

In the Old Testament, particularly in the Law of Moses, as expressed in the Book of Deuteronomy and the Book of Leviticus, there are three groups of people for whom Yah-

---

[13] Fr. Daniel Groody, CDC, Ph.D., *Crossing the Divide: Foundations of a Theology of Migration and Refugee* (South Bend, IN: University of Notre Dame, 2009).

weh wants the Israelites to show mercy and compassion: the orphan, the stranger, and the widow.

"For the Lord your God is God of Gods and Lord of Lords, the Great God, Mighty and awesome, who is not partial and takes no bride, who executes justice for the orphan and the widow, and who loves the strangers, providing them food and clothing. You shall also love the stranger, for you were strangers in the land of Egypt" (Deut. 10:17–19).

"You shall not strip your vineyard bare, or gather the fallen grapes of your vineyard; you shall leave them for the poor and the alien: I am the Lord your God" (Lev. 19:10), and "when an alien resides with you in your land, you shall not oppress the alien. The alien who resides with you shall be to you as the citizens among you; you shall love the alien as yourself, for you were aliens in the land of Egypt: I am the Lord your God" (Lev. 19:33–34).

As the history of salvation unfolds in sacred Scripture, wonderful things happen wherever hospitality is offered. In fact, salvation history begins with the hospitality of Abraham. Abraham and Sarah offered a sumptuous banquet to the three mysterious visitors whom Abraham recognized as a visit from the Lord. Because of that gesture of hospitality, Abraham and Sarah are promised a child, and the rest is history—salvation history, that is. Thus, the promise of God that Abraham was to be the father of the people of God is fulfilled.

In the Gospel stories as well, wonderful things happen whenever Jesus is offered hospitality—or offers hospitality. At the wedding feast at Cana, because of the hospitality offered to Jesus and his mother, a stunning miracle happens with water changed into choice wine. When the Samaritan woman is offered living water, she becomes the first evangelizer in the Gospel of John.

When Jesus hosts the five thousand and more on the other side of the Sea of Galilee, the five loaves and two fishes multiply in order to feed everyone with abundant leftovers for people to take home. When Jesus invites his apostles to the Last Supper, and they accept his invitation, he gives to all believers the gift of the Eucharist. Yes, when hospitality is offered, wonderful things happen.

Thus it is with immigrants: when our church and our country receive and welcome immigrants and refugees, we are blessed. Already we see this in the US church. New life, excitement, and hope are among the treasures new immigrants bring; many of them are Roman Catholic, and they are taking the place of the large numbers of those who left the church. A significant number of seminarians, young priests, and permanent deacons are immigrants or sons of immigrants.

The Historic Mass at
Los Dos Nogales in 2014

In early 2014, a group of US bishops went to the US–Mexican border at Nogales, Arizona, and Nogales, Sonora, Mexico, to celebrate a Mass to give attention to the need for comprehensive immigration reform. I was among the various bishops who celebrated the Eucharist. Cardinal Seán O'Malley of Boston was the main celebrant. The most moving moment was at communion when the bishops reached through the cracks of the steel fence to give communion to the people on the Mexican side of the border. Cardinal O'Malley compared our Mass at the border with Pope Francis's meeting with refugees at Lampedusa, Italy, in July 2013.

The choice of Lampedusa for his first official trip outside Rome was highly symbolic for the pontiff, who reveals high emotion when it comes to the pain of immigrants. He said that news reports of the deaths of desperate people trying to reach a better life had been like "a thorn in the heart." He referred to a selfish society that has slid into "the globalization of indifference."

"We have become used to other people's suffering, it doesn't concern us, it doesn't interest us, it's none of our business!" he said during his homily from an altar built from an old fishing boat.

He also had harsh words for human traffickers who he said profited from the misery of others and asked pardon for "those whose decisions at a global level have created the conditions that created this drama."

Pope Francis repeated some of these themes at a Mass held in Ciudad Juarez on February 17, 2016. His visit to Mexico was symbolic insofar as he visited two borders, the Mexican–Guatemalan border on the south, and the Mexican–American border on the north. He wanted to show support for those attempting to cross both borders.

Before the Mass in Ciudad Juárez, on the bank of the Rio Grande, he mounted a ramp, which was topped with a large black cross and three smaller ones as well as a pair of shoes. There he prayed for those immigrants who have died on their journey north. The entire crowd of over 250,000 people observed a reverent silence as the pope prayed before the cross. He then waved to those on the American side, some of whom were undocumented immigrants.

During his homily, Pope Francis decried "the human tragedy" that forces people to migrate, risking death, "each step a journey laden with grave injustices: the enslaved, the imprisoned, and the extorted. . . . Migrants are our brothers and sisters expelled by poverty and violence, trafficking; so many of these brothers and sisters of ours are the consequence of a trade in human beings. . . . Injustice is radicalized in the young; they are 'cannon fodder,' persecuted and threatened when they try to flee the spiral of violence and the hell of drugs."

As we bishops were being transported from the Mass, the smiling faces of the many thousands showed that in the pope's presence and his words, he did accomplish what he intended: to be a missionary of hope and peace.

At the Angelus, St. Peter's Square, on July 6, 2014, the pope said, "In the poorest countries, and also in the peripheral areas of the richest, there are many people who are weary and exhausted under the unbearable weight of abandonment and indifference. Indifference: How much damage human indifference causes to those in need! The indifference of Christians is worse. At the margins of society, many men and women are sorely tested by poverty, but also by dissatisfaction and frustration. Many are compelled to emigrate at risk of their own lives. Many more every day bear the weight of an economic system that exploits man and imposes an unbearable 'yoke' upon them that the privileged few do not want to carry. To each of these sons of the Father who is in heaven, Jesus says, 'Come to me, all of you'" (Matthew 11:28).

Chapter 7

Urgent Pastoral Concerns
in the Latino World

When I finished my undergraduate degree at the University of St. Thomas in Houston, Texas, I decided to join the priests who administered and taught at the university, the Congregation of the Priests of St. Basil, known as the Basilian Fathers. My attraction to the Basilians was the fact that they were both priests and teachers, and those were the two things that I wanted to be for the rest of my life.

I began my preparation at St. Basil's Novitiate in Pontiac, Michigan. Leaving Texas and going to Michigan was like going to a different country. Michigan was in many ways strange to me not only because of the climate but also their English style and, in those days, a lack of Latino cultural presence. One of the first things they taught us was how to eat, and for this, they took out a book by Emily Post and taught us many rules such as how to eat an apple at the table. The instructions were to cut it in pieces and eat the apple piece by piece. To eat bananas, we removed the peel with a knife and fork, and then with the knife cut the banana in small pieces to eat with a fork. (That is not the way to do it in Bay City, Texas!) We were never to place the knife in such a way that it formed a bridge between the table and the edge of the plate; the place for the knife was at the edge of the plate. They taught us to eat everything on the plate and not leave anything. It was also bad manners to eat a slice of bread without first cutting it into small pieces. They told us this was the best way to eat.

When I went on to continue studies in Canada, they abided by the same Emily Post eating rules. The Canadians also said, "This is the best way to eat." Later, I was assigned to Mexico, both to study and to do pastoral work. There were places in Mexico where there were neither knives nor forks, so we ate everything with a tortilla. They told us always to build a little bridge between the table and the edge of the plate with our knives. We were always to leave a bit of food on the plate, otherwise leaving the plate clean was like having made a pig out of ourselves. They told us that this was the best way to eat.

During a sabbatical to the East Asian Pastoral Institute in Manila, the Philippines, we traveled, on occasion, to the rural areas of the country. They would use a clean banana leaf for a plate. With washed hands, they would eat their rice and a piece of fish with their hands, and they told us, "This is the best way to eat."

When I visited missionaries in China and other Asian countries, they used chopsticks to eat and they told me, "This is the best way to eat."

When I returned to live and work in the United States, I went to my home state, Texas. In Texas, I relearned to eat the way I had been taught as a child, to eat the Mexican–American way, with a piece of tortilla in one hand and an American fork in the other and make little taquitos and eat the tortilla filled with food. My conclusion was, "Forget all the rest; this is the best way to eat!"

*   *   *

I use this story often to explain various things. First, there is no "best way to eat." There is no best language, or best cuisine, or best skin color. In the eyes of God, we are all loved the same, no matter what race or culture we claim as our own. I learned that we should respect other people's cultural styles and preferences, and be open to differences, and when we do this, we can enrich our lives with the diversity that surrounds us.

One of the valuable things in my priestly and bishop's life is to respect and carefully listen to others, even though sometimes their accent makes it difficult for me to understand them. At the missionary school in the Philippines, there were about ninety priests, women and men religious, and laypeople from about thirty different countries. The language used in classes and discussions was English, and some of our classmates did not speak the English language well. It was difficult to understand them when they spoke their version of English.

I realized, toward the end of the seven-month course, I had not been mixing with those who did not speak English well (in my estimation). I thought, "I must get to know these people." I invited a novice mistress from Indonesia to go for a walk with me so we could talk. Right away, I did all the talking and told her all the wonderful things I would do when I returned to missionary work in Mexico. Sister stopped me. "Ricardo, let me tell you something. Before you do, be."

These small little words taught me a great deal, especially that it is more important for me to be an authentic Christian. My mistake was avoiding this sister and others who spoke like her, and not expecting any wisdom to come from them. I learned that all people, no matter what or how they speak, have wisdom to offer; *accents* should not fool me. When I listen carefully to them, openly and with respect, I can learn something.

Welcoming the Latino Catholic

The reality of *church* comes to us in many different ways, but where church happens, where you feel it, where you see and touch it, is at the parish level. For me, the parish is where church happens. It is the parish where people encounter the body of Christ and Christ himself—that is, unless we place obstacles in the way of this blessed encounter.

A mission-driven parish and a maintenance parish differ. A mission-driven parish listens and responds to its people and serves their needs. A mission-driven parish is anxious to serve parishioners' needs beyond the spiritual. A maintenance-driven parish is limited to worship, sacramental preparation, and catechesis of children. Priorities include making sure there are enough funds to pay for the material upkeep of the parish plant and pay salaries.

So much depends on the theological mind of the pastor. If he is imbued with a Vatican II ecclesiology, he stresses the church as a servant one. Chances are the parish will be mission-driven and promote such activities as Alcoholics Anonymous and Al-Anon, provide early childhood education, conduct voter registration drives, be part of a community organization, and organize or contribute to charitable projects for the poor such as food banks and soup kitchens. A mission-driven parish can provide additional services such as marital and individual counseling. It will also reach out to parishioners who may be in jail or prison and their families. For immigrants, it could provide English as a Second Language as well as citizenship classes.

As a matter of course, mission-driven parishes practice hospitality. Earlier, I recounted how my grandparents felt so unwelcome at the one parish in Bay City. Had their faith not been strong, they would have left the church outright, but their faith instinct kept their hearts open to a better manifestation of church and Jesus Christ. Eventually this manifestation came when the Basilian missionaries arrived to serve at the little railroad car church, which served as the first Latino church in Bay City.

The church extends a special welcome to strangers who arrive at the doorstep of the church, confused, bewildered and intimidated by their new North American surroundings. The first rule of hospitality is to extend a warm welcome, not only to immigrants; others need to be welcomed as well.

A Latino friend of mine received a full scholarship to study law at Harvard University. When he arrived there, he may have been one of a handful of Latino students. He told me the only place he felt comfortable and found something from *back home* was in the Catholic Church. In the church, he was connected; there more than at any other place, he felt at home. At one of our best parishes in the Diocese of Las Cruces, the pastor and his pastoral team make it a point to invite all the new parishioners who came to this parish in the previous month to a meal. They call it "Breakfast with the Pastor."

Inviting new parishioners into the life of the parish as soon as possible is an indispensable part of hospitality. It is essential they feel included in all the worship and programs, especially in the formational ones. Newcomers ought to be included in the consultative bodies such as the parish and finance councils.

It is important, however, to avoid creating a parallel parish made up only of Latinos. It is true people feel at home with those experiencing the same things, and perhaps it will be acceptable for them to be part of the Latino makeup of the parish, but this should not continue indefinitely. There will be a time for the newly arrived Latino to become part of the larger makeup of the church. Occasions that promote unity in the diversity of the parish are parish spiritual retreats, presented bilingually, as well as the parish fiesta, where every group shares in the fund-raising as well as the social aspect of the fiesta. A parish could also organize sharing sessions where people tell their stories and their journeys of faith. Perhaps this could be part of the parish retreat. A parish comes alive by searching for ways to build up the community and celebrate its diversity rather than struggle with it.

A parish must never forget that the disabled and their caregivers are among its responsibilities. Pope Francis impresses the world with his style. On his arrival at any place, he first goes to those forgotten: the sick, the poor, the disabled, and the imprisoned. He sets a good example for our parish communities. It follows that our worship should always welcome the disabled, for example, by including ramps that allow those in wheelchairs or walkers to reach the sanctuary without difficulty so that they can participate as lectors, altar servers, and communion ministers. Signing should be available for the hearing impaired.

Religious education programs should be encouraged to use materials available for the preparation of disabled children for the reception of the sacraments. In some theaters, special earphones are available for the hearing impaired so that they can hear every word on the stage. Our parishes could do something similar for those of us who may have a hard time hearing.

Among the forgotten parishioners are the caregivers who tend to the needs of the disabled, the elderly, and their families. Some communities provide respite services whereby caregivers are offered a day off to tend to their personal needs, such as shopping, going to the beauty salon, or taking in a movie. Parishes can also offer spiritual retreats for caregivers. Parishes can bring in community experts to talk to caregivers about self-care and give them tips for providing quality care to their family members. Of course, in all cases, parishes should respect the language needs of their parishioners.

Prison and Jail Ministry

Latinos are overrepresented in prisons and jails, especially in areas of the US where Latinos make up a higher percentage of the population.

In the US Southwest, for example, Latinos may be the majority-incarcerated group in some cities and counties in Texas, California, Arizona, and New Mexico. It is not surprising that in some jails and prisons in the Southwest, the major religious affiliation represented among Latinos is often Roman Catholic. Unfortunately, there are not enough Catholic prison and jail ministers, and some of these are not Spanish speakers.

Over the past eleven years, there has been a dramatic rise among Latinos in federal prisons. Before the law was changed, an unauthorized immigrant could have as many as forty contacts with the Border Patrol and not be charged with a crime; now a second or subsequent contact with the Border Patrol—that is, being caught entering illegally—will result in a felony charge, and before deportation, incarceration for anywhere from one to six months. According to a Pew Research study, "The total number of offenders sentenced in federal courts more than doubled from 1991 to 2007. During this period, the number of sentenced offenders who were Hispanic nearly quadrupled and accounted for more than half (54%) of the growth in the total number of sentenced offenders."

Evangelical and other non-Catholic ministers abound in our prisons and greatly outnumber Catholic ministers. The priest shortage exacerbates the problem. A major prison in New Mexico offers Mass and confessions only twice a year, even though lay ministers make weekly visits. It happens all too often that Latinos enter a jail or prison as Catholics, but they leave as Protestant Evangelicals.

In 2000, the US bishops' conference published one of its most important pastoral statements, "Responsibility, Rehabilitation and Restoration: A Catholic Perspective on Crime and Criminal Justice."[1] The statement describes the huge problem

---

[1] United States Conference of Catholic Bishops, "Responsibility, Rehabilitation and Restoration: A Catholic Perspective on Crime and Criminal Justice"

our country faces in terms of not only crimes committed but also the challenges of incarceration and the need to reform our criminal justice system. Much of what the bishops said then remains true now. There is an overrepresentation of minorities among the incarcerated, most of whom have not committed violent crimes, whose offenses are alcohol- and drug-related. What many of these people need is rehabilitation programs to remove them from their addictions.

The US bishops devote much attention in their statement to *restorative justice*. Restorative justice seeks to repair damage, (re)establish dignity, and (re)integrate all who are harmed and alienated, including the perpetrator as well as victims. The involvement of the victims in the healing process is the essence of restorative justice. In our statement, the US bishops say that we must work for healing for everyone impacted by crime, including offenders, victims of crime, and communities, and with special consideration for how crime and sentencing affect families. In the statement, we also call for a reform of the criminal justice system to promote the common good and that punishment has a constructive and redemptive purpose. We also address the growing prison population that disproportionately affects minorities and poor people.

This document should be required study for seminarians, permanent deacons, and lay ministers. Prison and jail ministry is ideal for those called to the permanent diaconate and can be an invaluable service in the cause of restorative justice.

When Pope Francis visited the prison in Ciudad Juárez, a female inmate addressed him in the name of all the incarcerated. For me, it was one of the most emotional and touching moments in the pope's visit to Mexico. What she said is a good example of what we mean by restorative justice. After

(November 15, 2000), http://www.usccb.org/issues-and-action/human-life-and-dignity/criminal-justice-restorative-justice/crime-and-criminal-justice.cfm.

mentioning that at times they feel hopeless and sad, she said, "There is no greater treasure than to have human contact with our loved ones." She went on to say that even though they have broken the law, most inmates have the hope of redemption, and some have the will to attain it. The time in prison does not mean that all has ended for them. It is just a pause in their lives, a time to reflect on how they want to live their lives and what they want for their children.

She ended her message to the pope with these words:

> Fellow inmates, let us do all we can so that our children will not repeat our history. Personally, the great blessing that I have is to see my daughter grow and see her change into a big girl, with her beautiful long hair, and with those big eyes that I am able to see every time the prison door opens in order to let her in. My daughter's smile and seeing her run to my arms return life to me and to hear, "I love you, Mom," from her lips gives me strength with which I can survive whatever time I have in jail.

In some places, inmates connect with their home parishes and families before they leave the prison so that, when they do leave, they will have a support system that will help them reenter civil society as well as the church. When parishes reach out to families in need, families of inmates should be included, and those families should receive a special welcome in all our parishes. Catholic organizations ought to reach out to those who are in halfway houses and, in many of our cities, to those in Dismas Charities. Catholic businesspersons should be open to employing former inmates wherever possible.

At the present time, the United States Conference of Catholic Bishops, through the Committee on Domestic Justice and Human Development, is urging Congress to support sentencing reform by adopting the Smarter Sentencing Act (HR 3382/S. 1410) and restorative justice efforts as part of the Second Chance Act (S 1690/HR 3465).

Domestic Violence

Domestic violence is a pervasive problem in society, not only a Latino problem; it transcends culture and socioeconomic classes, and it must be addressed. Among Latinos, victims of domestic violence (usually women) do not report cases to the authorities, especially if the victims are undocumented.

Several years ago, I wrote a pastoral letter titled "Speaking the Unspeakable" on the issue of domestic violence.[2] Some of the following points are from that letter, which was preceded by countless consultations with victims and perpetrators of domestic violence, law enforcement officers, district attorneys, judges, pastors, and caseworkers.

Domestic violence manifests in various forms: degrading comments, manipulation of financial resources to intimidate, the use of physical strength to bully, and ultimately, to injure or kill. These are only a few in a long list of its manifestations. The form may vary, but the result is the same. Domestic violence exchanges the natural bonds of love and nurturing for the unnatural relationships of aggressors trampling mercilessly on the dignity, rights, and aspirations of those they promise to love and cherish.

The nature of domestic violence has been a tragic element in the evolution of the world's civilizations and continues to be a plague of epidemic proportions. Many people

---

[2] Rev. Ricardo Ramírez, C.S.B., "Speaking the Unspeakable: A Pastoral Letter on Domestic Violence" (July 6, 2001), http://www.latinodv.org/docs/SpeakingTheUnspeakable.pdf.

in our society have experienced and continue to experience the terror of living in danger of attack by another family member. For generations, violence in the home was common and went virtually unchallenged. It took courageous women and men to bring the ugly reality of domestic violence into the public forum.

The plague of violence in the home is a learned behavior and passes on from one generation to the next. Alcohol or drugs often trigger this learned behavior. We know little about the treatment and prevention of domestic violence. We tend to oversimplify the problem by reducing violence in the home to economic and/or social pressures that create stress within the family unit. Such is not the case. Perpetrators and victims come from every walk of life, from the poorest to the richest, and from the social outcasts to the most respected citizens of our communities. There is still much that we do not know about domestic violence.

Compounding the situation is the fact that children residing in homes where domestic violence occurs are previous victims of physical or sexual abuse about half of the time. The night terrors and other horrors experienced by children contribute to life-long difficulties with self-esteem.

Tolerating and minimizing domestic violence has to stop. Victims are thinking, feeling, and frightened individuals. Domestic violence will not end until the issue is uprooted from our culture, which often justifies and glorifies violence.

We must confront domestic violence, which is a shameful exercise of power against lives entwined by ties of blood and family. We join with the bishops of the United States and other groups believing "violence in any form—physical, sexual, psychological, or verbal—is sinful; many times, it is a crime as well." Domestic violence is never justified, for it sacrilegiously fouls the sacred covenanted relationships of marriage.

Our pastoral experience tells us that not only in the past, but even today, spouses—most often women—are exhorted over and over to forgive and forget spousal abuse. At times, clergy tell the abused to return to marital life. Thus, they are subject to further victimization. In doing so, clergy fail to acknowledge and validate the experience of victims. Well-meaning as they may be, these pastoral ministers do not recognize the insidious nature of domestic violence as emanating from a culture and an environment of domination and subordination. To encourage a victim to return to such an environment without the benefit of qualified professional help is irresponsible. When such errors occur, or sinful actions are excused in God's name, the consequences are even more tragic.

We recognize that all too often Scripture is used incorrectly to justify husbands dominating their wives. Such is the case with the passage found in St. Paul's letter to the Ephesians: "Wives be submissive to your husbands" (Eph. 5:22). This passage, which was shaped by its times and culture, reflects the highly hierarchical household that was part of the Greco–Roman Empire in which St. Paul was writing. In that society, just as slaves had to submit to their masters, so, too, wives had to submit to their husbands. Fortunately, ours is a different cultural setting wherein all people are equal. The context of St. Paul's message, however, exhorts husbands and, indeed, all spouses to love one another as Christ loves the church (Eph. 5:25). In Christian marriage, spouses give their lives for one another as Christ gave his life for the church. Husbands and wives love each other in a way in which they consider and treat each other as equals. This is the Gospel mandate.

The home is the privileged place to form our hearts and minds in a way that Christian virtue will develop. Respect for the dignity of the other person must be the foundation stone toward all moral formation. We all pray that there be peace in the world, but that peace should have as its wellspring peace and respect in the family. Peace is not only the absence of physical violence but also the absence of harsh words, the raising of voices, passive-aggressiveness, and other forms of violence, including sexual abuse. Recourse to violence is not something we are born with; like racism, it is something that we acquire along the way, often through a child's observation of what goes on in his or her surroundings.

A practical suggestion would be that the issue of domestic violence always be included in marriage preparation, in Confirmation classes, and in safe environment sessions. Of utmost importance is educating of all those involved in pastoral ministry to respond with spiritual, practical, and compassionate support that will best assist victims and perpetrators of domestic violence. Parishes can establish networks with legal, medical, and civic communities uniting our energies to support continuing changes in public opinion and policy. It is of the utmost importance that we, as a church community, recognize and challenge the culture of violence and degradation of all people as promoted through the irresponsible use of the Internet, television, film, entertainment industry, and our own behavior.

Movements

All pastoral concerns require people who are filled with enthusiasm for the work of the church and imbued with spiritual energy. The liturgy is at the heart of the life of the parish, but there are other things that effectively move hearts and minds to Jesus Christ. These are apostolic movements such as Cursillos, ACTS, Engaged and Marriage Encounter, Youth Encuentros, and the Charismatic Movement. Not as well known is *Talleres de Oración y Vida*, following the spirituality of

Father Ignacio Larrañaga. It is a fifteen-week course involving two-hour sessions weekly, and it teaches people how to pray and how to live lives that reflect their prayers.

Today, one of the greatest contributions stems from the Catholic biblical movement, and numerous parishes enjoy Catholic study of the Bible throughout the country; many of these are offered in both English and Spanish. Small Christian communities have met with success in many of our Latino parishes.

Chapter 8

Faith Expressions at the Margins

My grandmother, Francisca Espitia, was one of the women who lived out in the South Texas ranches and who would grab a rattlesnake by the tail and snap its head off. We called my grandmother Panchita. She was strong, loving, and wise, and with those personal gifts she raised a big family.

When I was asked to be an auxiliary bishop in San Antonio, and knew that there was going to be a reception for me, I called my grandmother Panchita. The reception was to take place in San Antonio, Texas, about two hundred miles from Panchita's home in Houston. So the ninety-year-old woman took the bus, alone, to be with her grandson.

Well, two or three days before the party, my grandmother arrived. She called me from the bus station in San Antonio and said, "Come, son, pick me up at the Greyhound." I asked her why she had arrived days before the party. She said that she didn't want to be late. I asked her if she had come alone. Her answer was, "Oh, there were a lot of people on the bus!"

My mother joined us the next day, and we borrowed some elegant evening gowns for them to wear to the party. I even sent them to have their hair done at the beauty salon. The evening of the party, the two women looked elegant, and while we were waiting for our ride, and just to make conversation, I asked, "Grandmother, what have you been doing lately?" She said, "I've been having a good time."

"Wow! At ninety years old, what do you do to have a good time?"

"Oh son, I have been going to funerals."

I said, "You have been having a good time at funerals?"

"Oh yes. Yes, we drink coffee, we tell stories, we meet old friends—it is wonderful. We have a great time."

I said, "Grandma, how can you have a good time when somebody dies?"

She looked at me, straight into my eyes, and with a look of seriousness in her face, and with a hint of scolding me, she said, "Son, haven't you learned yet that it is a privilege to die?"

In all my years of studying theology and listening to sermons, I had never quite heard it that way. A few weeks later, she had that privilege.

After being ordained a bishop, I went to see her in the hospital, recovering from a heart attack. We knew she probably would not make it at her age. I'll never forget what she kept repeating, like a mantra, "Solo quiero ver a Dios" (I just want to see the face of God).

That was the last thing I ever heard her say. She had the privilege to die two days later.

When she was dying, she sang religious songs from our childhood, especially "Al cielo, Al cielo, Al cielo quiero ir" (To heaven, to heaven; I want to go to heaven).

She died singing. She was just an amazing woman. I will never forget Panchita.[1]

*   *   *

---

[1] Bishop Ricardo Ramírez, *Stories, Old Friends, a Good Time 'Til the End*, NPR's Story Corps (June 29, 2012), http://www.npr.org/2012/06/29/155913610/stories-old-friends-a-good-time-til-the-end.

In the early years of my priesthood, I worked as a missionary in rural Mexico, in places where the Catholic faith runs very deep. In Mexico, as throughout Latin America, popular religion is part of the fabric of the faith of the church. Traditions abound throughout the church year and, most often, during the Advent and Christmas seasons. In this chapter, a partial list of the many expressions of popular religiosity among Latinos is included.

As a seminarian in Mexico, I recall a very beautiful Christmas Midnight Mass. In Mexico, there is a custom of *la acostada del niño*, the laying of the baby Jesus in the crib. The ritual takes place in the homes, where the extended family, including the *padrinos* (the godparents or sponsors of the celebration) of the Child Jesus, gathers to celebrate Christmas.

It was my first Christmas in Mexico, and the experience was memorable. Every family in the village brought its small, doll-like image of the child Jesus. What a sight it was! There were hundreds of statues of the baby Jesus all around the altar. The people told us they "wanted to make sure baby Jesus attended Mass." After Mass, each family took their baby Jesus and left the church.

We priests ran up to the roof to watch an unforgettable scene. It was a foggy night, yet we could see small family groups walking back to their homes with lighted candles and singing lullabies to the Christ child. They were literally taking Jesus home with them. Now I preach about the Eucharist using as an example the Mexican Christmas custom: at the end of every Eucharist, we are called to take Jesus with us to our homes and everywhere else.

El Día de los Muertos in Mexico is celebrated everywhere, and some of those practices have been exported to the United States. In this country, the Day of the Dead is commemorated in a more humorous and farcical way and mixed with

Halloween customs. In Mexico, it is of utmost importance that the entire family gathers on November 2, All Souls Day. Even if they live far away from their ancestral home, they will travel many hours on buses and other vehicles; many will make the sacrifice of paying airfare to be present with the rest of the family in honor of their dead.

At the home, an altar for the dead is assembled, and photographs of the deceased family members are placed together with food, drink (sometimes tequila), and copious flowers, including the *cempasúchitl*, the Aztec name for flower of the dead, which we know as marigolds. It is interesting to note that this flower happens to be abundant in the season of autumn. When the flower dies and breaks apart, each petal is a seed; each flower holds hundreds of seeds, and with each tiny seed is the promise of new and abundant life. The folk belief is that the dead will come the eve of November 2 and will eat the food placed on the altar (the next day the living will actually eat the food).

On November 2, the family goes to the graves of their deceased, cleans them, and places fresh flowers and, again, the *cempasúchitl*. The family prays at the graves and sometimes asks the parish cantor to sing special hymns in honor of the dead. Throughout the community, special foods, such as *mole* (a special chili sauce, which incorporates many spices, grains, and chocolate, often served over chicken) and bread of the dead (*pan de muerto*), are served. The *pan de muerto* is usually decorated with sugar bones. Friends exchange *calaveras,* or miniature skulls, made with sugar. While it is a sad occasion that their loved ones are gone, faith in the new life of the resurrection is celebrated, so a festive ambience prevails.

These stories point to the phenomenon of popular religiosity, which is alive in the minds and hearts of Latino people from all cultural backgrounds. Every Latino group, from whatever place of origin, has its rich and diverse religious traditions that have a profound effect on the faith of the people. Popular religiosity cannot be disregarded in the task of evangelizing or reevangelizing the Latino.

What is popular religiosity? The final document from the Third General Conference of the Latin American Bishops held in Puebla, Mexico, in 1979 gives this definition:

> By the religion of the people, popular religiosity or popular piety, we mean the whole complex of underlying beliefs rooted in God, the basic attitudes that flow from these beliefs, and the expressions that manifest them. It is the form of cultural life that religion takes on among a given people. . . . It is the religion of the people of Latin America, an expression of their Catholic faith. It is a people's Catholicism. (*Puebla* no. 444)

Among Latinos, there exists an innate tendency to create a way to arrive at divine transcendence. In popular religion, the human imagination finds an approach to the divine by means of customs, traditions, and faith expressions. Pastoral theologians refer to this phenomenon as a manner of enculturation. According to St. John Paul II, "Given that in America, popular piety is a mode of enculturation of the Catholic faith and has often assumed indigenous religious forms, we must not underestimate the fact that, prudently considered, it too can provide valid cues for a more complete enculturation of the Gospel" (*Ecclesia in America* no. 16). The people of the Americas manage to pass on their faith from generation to generation through popular religion. This is one of the more successful ways of transmitting their faith. Popular religion in its faith expressions give meaning to life with all the challenges, difficulties, and demands that we face in being born and in dying; in all that is good and all that is bad; successes and failures; health and illness.

Some look upon practices of popular religion as excesses, which they view as distancing the people from the official church, and the sacraments. At times, the power that popular religion brings to the process of evangelization is disregarded. Pope Paul VI teaches in *Evangelii Nuntiandi* (no. 48), "These expressions were for a long time regarded as less pure and were sometimes despised, but today they are almost everywhere being rediscovered." He calls for the "proper attitude in regard to this reality, which is at the same time so rich and so vulnerable."

Rather than alienating people from real-life challenges, such as social and economic realities, they can contribute enormously toward bringing people together in their struggle for justice and freedom. Such is the case, for example, in Mexico when the people united for independence from Spain under the banner of Our Lady of Guadalupe. The same has happened with the farmworker movement in the United States.

Popular Practices Connected with the Sacraments

In the family celebrations of baptism and matrimony, popular practices prevail. In my view, they serve to bring out the richness of the sacramental life and engage the people in a deep way with the sacramental encounters with Christ. The following are but a few of the many expressions of faith that are traditional to Latino families.

People recognize the fact of begetting and giving birth to children as a wonderful treasure from God. The selection of godparents is important because a reverent relationship between the parents and the godparents is established for the rest of their lives. There is even an untranslatable word used to name the relationship between the parents and the godparents, *comadre* and *compadre*. The bond between godparents and their godchildren is one of lifelong respect. Godchildren look up to their godparents as they go through life, and when the bond is nurtured, the godparents become part of the family of their godchildren.

At times, the godparents dress the child in his or her baptismal clothes, or are responsible for purchasing the baptismal outfit. Baptism in New Mexico is followed by a home ritual in which the godparents present the newly baptized child to his or her parents. As they do so, they say, "*Compadre y comadre: les entregamos esta rosa que salió con los santos sacramentos y el agua que recibió; se llama _____*" (*Compadre and comadre*, we give you this rose that came from the Holy Sacraments and from the water received; his/her name is _____). The parents accept the child, saying, "*Recibimos esta rosa que de la Iglesia salió con los santos sacramentos y el agua que recibió. Gracias.*"

Folk customs surrounding the sacrament of matrimony can vary from place to place. For example, the custom of formally requesting the hand of the bride in marriage, *pedir la mano,* is still practiced. Sometimes a priest is asked to serve as proxy for the bridegroom when visiting the parents of the bride in order to accomplish this delicate task. This family custom is done out of respect of the future bridegroom for his bride-to-be and her parents. In New Mexico when the request is refused, there is what is called giving *calabasas* (pumpkins or squash). When the bride's hand is given, new relations begin between the two families. The two sets of parents become *compadres* and *comadres,* becoming part of each other's extended family. Those relationships are treasured with utmost endearment and respect.

At the wedding, *arras* (thirteen gold or silver coins) are given by the groom to the bride as a sign that nothing will be lacking in their home. Today when both husband and wife work in order to keep up the home, the *arras* can be exchanged as a sign that each will share all things. The *lazo* or *prendorio* sometimes takes the form of a large rosary placed over the shoulders of the bride and groom. Other times the *prendorio* is made with real or imitation orange blossoms. The *lazo* signifies the yoke of marriage and the bond of love that unites their lives. The bride brings an extra flower bouquet, the extra one she places at the altar of the Blessed Virgin. The role of the members of the wedding party, or *padrinos*, varies. For example, they may be asked to help with the wedding expenses, so they can be a *padrino* for the rings, the flowers, the *lazo*, the *arras*, and for the reception. Often the custom is for the bride and groom to receive a blessing from their parents at the beginning of the Nuptial Mass.

Popular Practices Connected to Devotions

The basic truths of Catholicism are honored through deep-seated devotions. Among these are devotions to the Trinity, especially in making the sign of the cross. The thumb and index finger form a cross, which represents Jesus who saved us, while the other three fingers represent the three divine persons, the Father, the Son, and the Holy Spirit. At the end of the signing of the cross, the person will kiss the cross, which is formed by the thumb and the index finger as a gesture of belief in both the Trinity and Jesus on the cross as our salvation. This simple gesture teaches very simply about our basic beliefs: the Trinity, the incarnation, and our salvation on the cross.

Devotions to Jesus Christ can vary from region to region. In many places and during Holy Week, Jesus in his passion is revered with the title *El Nazareno*. His statue is crowned with thorns, dressed with a purple cloth, and girdled with a rope, showing the wounds of the scourging, and has been popular in devotions since the early days of evangelization in America.

Extremely popular is the devotion to Jesus in his childhood with the title *El Santo Niño* and *El Santo Niño de Atocha*. The myth connected with this devotion dates back to the time of the Moorish occupation of Spain. Christians were often imprisoned, and the only visit they were allowed was children who would bring them food. The story is told that at *Atocha*, a central *barrio* in Madrid, Spain, a young child would come to the prison with a breakfast of bread and a gourd full of water. As he fed the prisoners, his basket and gourd were still full; they were never empty. The child would bless the imprisoned before he left. The image of *El Santo Niño* is represented with a gourd and a seashell. This devotion is continued in Chimayó, New Mexico, where there is also devotion to the black Christ on the cross, similar to one venerated in Esquipulas, Guatemala.

A favorite image of Christ among Latinos is of the sacred heart. The sacred heart is the symbol of Christ's eternal love for each one of us and expresses his kindness and mercy. Some families enthrone the image of the sacred heart in their homes or on their vehicles. Similar to the devotion to the sacred heart is that of the divine mercy made popular by St. John Paul II who honored the apparitions of Jesus as divine mercy to St. Faustina in Poland.

Also in Northern New Mexico, where the village of Chimayó is located, there is devotion to Jesus with the title of *Nuestro Padre, Jesús Nazareno*. A centuries-old fraternity, *Los Penitentes*, is dedicated to meditation on the passion of Jesus and is accompanied by acts of penance, including the infliction of physical pain.

Another popular devotion to Jesus Christ is to Cristo Rey or Christ the King. This devotion is relatively new; in the twentieth century, "¡Viva Cristo Rey!" was the rallying cry of the *Cristero* rebellion in Mexico.

At the spot where three states come together, Chihuahua (Mexico), Texas, and New Mexico, a huge statue of Christ the King was dedicated in 1940 on Mount Cristo Rey; it is the site of one of the largest gatherings of Catholics in the Southwest. The gathering is always held on the last Sunday of October every year, and anywhere from twenty to thirty thousand people climb the mountain. On D-Day, June 6, 1944, the people of El Paso and Ciudad Juárez, Mexico, stormed the mountain to pray for safety of their relatives and friends involved in the European campaign. Devotion to Christ the King in the Southwest was brought to the United States by the Mexican Catholics fleeing the violent turmoil during the persecution of the church in the 1920s.

Adoration of the Blessed Sacrament has also been popular among the Latino people for generations. Young and old Latinos are attracted to this devotion, which is one of the highlights of devotions connected with Holy Week on Holy Thursday. This devotion is an indication of the people's faith in the real presence of Christ in the Eucharist.

Popular Devotions to the Blessed Virgin

The object of the greatest devotion to Mary among Latinos throughout the United States is to Our Lady of Guadalupe. I will devote the next chapter to this devotion. St. John Paul II at the Synod for America in 1997, recognizing this rich devotion, mandated that throughout the hemisphere of America the Mass in honor of Our Lady of Guadalupe would be celebrated from then on.

Nuestra Señora de San Juan de los Lagos is also a popular devotion in the US Southwest. This devotion stems from central Mexico, in the state of Jalisco, where a shrine and basilica are located. The first miracle ascribed to her intercession dates back to 1632. Estimations are that between seven and nine million people make pilgrimages to her every year. The image is a small statue, probably carved in the neighboring state of Michoacán and brought to San Juan in the early seventeenth century.

It is interesting to note that many Mexicans living in the United States, especially in Texas, would make promises to visit the shrine in Jalisco, but because of immigration obstacles, they were unable to make the journey. The Oblate Missionaries of Mary Immaculate built a church in her honor in San Juan, Texas, near Brownsville, close to the Mexican border. At the church, they are able to fulfill their promise without having to cross the border. This is a popular shrine that farmworkers visit before they begin their journeys in search of work in the United States.

Mary has many titles that are popular among Latinos of various cultural backgrounds. *La Purísima Concepción, La Inmaculada*, and *Nuestra Señora del Carmen* are favorite titles in New Mexico. Many Latinos wear a brown scapular in honor of Our Lady of Mount Carmel. Those of Cuban heritage honor *Nuestra Señora de la Caridad del Cobre*, while Puerto Ricans refer to *Nuestra Señora de la Divina Providencia*. Parallel with the devotion to the suffering Christ is that of Our Lady of Sorrows, or *Nuestra Señora de los Dolores*. She also goes by the title of *Nuestra Señora de la Soledad*, honored by people in Los Angeles. Every Latino country in the Western Hemisphere has a special devotion to the Blessed Virgin Mary under a special title. When published, the long-delayed Roman Missal in Spanish for use in the United States will include Mass texts for every one of these devotions, if they are not listed in the universal calendar.

Popular Devotions to the Saints

As with all Catholics, the saints are important for Latinos; we refer to our connection with them as the "communion of saints." *Lumen Gentium* (no. 49) says, "Being more closely united to Christ, those who dwell in heaven fix the whole Church more firmly in holiness. . . . They do not cease to intercede with the Father for us." For Latinos, appealing to the saints comes easily, since, in their minds, the saints seem to be approachable to all. They serve as credible role models on the journey of faith.

The one to whom we can go and through whose intercession anything is possible is *el Señor San José*. *San Antonio de Padua* is the saint who intercedes to find lost items. *San Martín de Porres* is a favorite of the poor and the humble, and as a friend of little animals. *San Martín Caballero* is the patron of business establishments and serves as a reminder to treat the poor with dignity and respect as *San Martín* did. *San Judas* is popular in cases of extreme need and impossible cases. *San Lorenzo* is also recognized as the saint of the poor because when he was asked by the Roman emperor to bring all the treasures of the church to him, San Lorenzo brought the poor and said, "These are the treasures of the Church." *San Pascual Baylon* is the patron saint of cooks. *Santa Teresa de Ávila* is invoked by those suffering from headaches, in particular migraines, and by students. *Santa Teresita del Niño Jesús* is the patroness of missions and religious novices. *Santa Rita* is a source of comfort for women who suffer domestic violence. *Santa Cecilia* is a favorite of musicians. Those in the media and the blind intercede to *Santa Clara*. *Santa Rosa de Lima* is the patroness of Latin America. *Santa Ana* and *San Joaquín* are models for grandparents.

Popular Practices Calling for Protection

Blessings still prevail among Catholic Latinos. Most of these blessings are invocations to God for protection and safety. The most common is the blessing given by parents to their children, at bedtime, when they leave the home either for part of the day or for longer times such as when they go away to college or to the service. At a wedding, the children about to be married are blessed by their parents. If possible, children are blessed by their dying parents.

On certain occasions, people request blessings from the priest. The priest blesses sick people, especially small children, and those leaving on a journey. People seeking a blessing can be experiencing fear, anxiety, or depression. On the Feast of St. Francis of Assisi, the priest blesses animals of all kinds. Blessed also are vehicles, homes, places of business, and other places of labor.

Positive Aspects of Popular Religiosity

Popular religiosity occupies a prominent place in the spirituality of Latinos regardless of their place of origin, including Latinos born in the United States. It is a spirituality imagined, developed, and continued by the laity, which gives identity to a community and helps maintain it. There is a fraternal spirit around devotions that transcends social class and creates a sense of solidarity among the people. The presence of the divine is perceived in devotions, and the presence of Christ is felt at Christmas, Palm Sunday, Good Friday, at Eucharist, and at holy places.

There is a great love of Mary, the mother of Jesus, and saints are viewed as protectors. Religious devotions create an awareness of the dignity of the human being and an awareness of sin and the need for atonement. There is a respect for life and concern for the dead. Devotions develop an appreciation of pilgrimage as symbolic of the journey of life in faith and cultivate the capacity to survive hardships and suffering with faith. Popular religious devotions allow people to express themselves through song, gesture, and dance.

The religion of the people can be a means of evangelization. It can lead to conversion, renewal, sanctification, reconciliation, and the strengthening of the community. The expressions of faith of the people accomplish what the official liturgy and the official doctrine of the church are sometimes not able to communicate. For example, on Good Friday, the dramatic portrayal of the Passion often conveys a much more powerful message than the official liturgy of the day. These expressions of faith help to develop respect for priests and religious as representatives of God. Finally, these devotions help people make prayer a part of everyday life and embrace the value of prayer.

Negative Aspects of Popular Religiosity

There can also be a negative side to popular religiosity. There can be a tendency toward superstition, magic, fatalism, fetishism, and ritualism. Sometimes there is an affinity to the past without being open to something new. There can be a false union of pagan and Christian ritual or rituals without appropriate formation. There is a danger that faith can be seen as a mere contract with God, and at times, there can be unnecessary and exorbitant expenses surrounding a devotion.

The temptation is to judge and to negate the possibility that these devotions can be authentic experiences of God. The measure of authenticity is in the Gospel and in the tradition of the church. *Ecclesia in America* (no. 16) says that popular piety, if properly directed, contributes to growth in the awareness of belonging to the church. It can nurture faith and offers the possibility of a valid response to the challenges of secularization.

The Pilgrimage as a Means of Evangelization

The pilgrimage is an experience available to all, without the restrictions of rules and regulations, and done in the way the pilgrim feels most comfortable. It enables the believer to have a faith experience independent of a cleric and involves people in a total flow that links them with all those past generations who have handed on the tradition.

The pilgrims are motivated to bring to God or to his representative the best of what they are or possess. More than anything, pilgrims bring a block of time, set aside from the routine of things, consecrated as a time of grace that places all other agendas on a lower priority. The design of the pilgrimage project is created by the pilgrims themselves; they alone determine the parameters of the pilgrimage, its form, pace, and length.

Authentic pilgrimage is an example of what religious anthropologists refer to as the process of liminality, the state and process of midtransition in a rite of passage—or, to use more traditional terminology, in the process of conversion.[2]

Pilgrimages follow the paradigm of the Way of the Cross, whereby Jesus willingly accepted the will of God to die for the salvation of others. It is in this light that the sacrifice and journey involved in pilgrimage find their meaning. Jesus has established the model of behaving according to the will of God. The pilgrimage can be more than a simple pious action;

[2] Victor Turner and Edith Turner, *Image and Pilgrimage in Christian Culture* (New York: Columbia University Press, 1978), 9, 57, 249.

it can be an exteriorized expression of mystical experience: "If mysticism is an interior pilgrimage, pilgrimage is an exteriorized mysticism."[3]

The Experience of Pilgrimage

God's revelation occurs in the lives of people during moments of crisis. There are moments when believers sense a deep need to touch the sacred and to sense that they are touched by God either directly or through one of his instruments.

At such times, people—for example, Latin Americans in both North and South America—have the custom of making *mandas,* or promises to God, to the Virgin, or to some saint for deliverance from a crisis. The *manda* can take many different forms: it can be the promise of a pilgrimage and an amount of money taken to the shrine or center of popular Catholicism. A *manda* can be a promise to wear the habit of St. Martín de Porres or Our Lady of Mt. Carmel. In the case of a woman, she can promise not to cut her hair. A man may promise not to shave off his beard for a certain length of time.

The first stage of pilgrimage then is the significant human experience through which we hear God. It is a call to sacred action but one with an open end; people enter the process not knowing where it will lead or what will happen to them. The pilgrims are aware, however, that the pilgrimage will release them temporarily from the ordinary structured life of work, play, home, and church. The pilgrim state is a privileged moment in the life of the Christian because there is an inward disposition to conversion, to deeper commitment to family and community. Miracles are not always expected, although they are sometimes sought.

---

[3] Ibid., 7.

The crisis moment is the immediate reason for deciding to undergo a pilgrimage. The person knows of a place he or she regards as the most sacred place to go, in order to pay the *manda*. That place is the holy *morada* or dwelling place of the divine. God is there, and there the pilgrim must go. It is at this decisive juncture that the person turns to God through the crucified Lord, the Virgin, or a saint.

During the journey, the pilgrim undergoes a stage of self-judgment and reassessment of his or her past life. In the midst of walking, traveling, praying along the way, or just plain thinking, the pilgrim, away from the routine of ordinary life, is able to objectify more clearly where he or she has been, as well as the present state of affairs, and can look to the future with more optimism.

Reassessment of one's life in the course of the pilgrimage is part of the overall conversion experience of the pilgrim. There may or may not be a sacramental confession at the end of the pilgrimage, but at least there will be a personal, albeit private, recognition of past transgressions and a desire to amend one's life and to take on one's responsibilities with greater seriousness.

The climax to the entire pilgrimage event is the celebrative moment at the shrine. The goal is reached; the task is accomplished. The summit of the mountain has been climbed. Often a genuine mystical experience occurs at this point, when the pilgrim is physically present at the holy place. It is holy ground, and the atmosphere provokes deep emotions on the part of the pilgrim.

People have told me that it was a moment of exceeding joy and emotion when they arrived at the shrine during Mass. It was not an ordinary Mass for them; it was a special moment of being lifted up and feeling the presence of God.

Various tangible things can happen to symbolize the internal personal disposition of devotion, feeling, and commitment. Things like bouquets or wreaths of flowers can be presented to the object of devotion; religious articles, such as rosaries, scapulars, crucifixes, or saints' statues, are brought as if to receive a blessing. Sometimes letters describing a favor bestowed are presented at the shrine; often candles are lit; in many places in Latino America, the holy place is approached on one's knees; indigenous peoples who have maintained their cultural expressions bring the dances, which they perform, outside the shrine in full folk costume.

The visit to the shrine lasts several hours; sometimes pilgrims spend the night. They will sleep outside if necessary. In Las Cruces on the eve of the Feast of Our Lady of Guadalupe, pilgrims climb Tortugas Mountain. It is an age-old tradition that is observed by hundreds of people each year. When they reach the top, they may choose to go to confession or visit with relatives and friends, some of whom they only see at this annual fiesta. At midday, the Eucharist is celebrated, usually with the bishop present. They share food and drink. They will spend the rest of the day on the mountain, until they process back to the church.

Ex-votos presented to the object of veneration can take a variety of forms. They can be drawings or primitive paintings depicting the miracle that Our Lord or a saint performed. There can be a diploma, a medal, or a trophy representing some achievement; married couples might leave their wedding photographs; sports teams might bring their uniforms in appreciation for having won a championship; a cured person might leave crutches, back braces, and the like.

While at the shrine, the pilgrims purchase articles that will serve as more than souvenirs. They will return home with religious articles that are symbols of a significant sojourn in their total Christian experience. These objects will serve as reminders of where they went, and that they touched God and God touched them.

The Novena as a
Celebration of Communion

The idea of the novena probably has its origins in early Greek and Roman customs performed by families. It consists of nine days of mourning after the death of a loved one, followed by a feast. Christians associate the number nine with the nine months Jesus spent in the womb, the giving up of his spirit at the ninth hour, and the number of days between the Ascension of Jesus and the coming of the Holy Spirit during which time the Blessed Virgin Mary prayed with the Apostles.

The novena for a great number of Catholics is another paradigm of religious behavior that can place the person in prayer on the threshold of conversion or at least to a deeper relationship to God. The nine days after or before a specific pivotal point in a person's life could be considered a pilgrimage in the general sense; novenas are journeys, which have a beginning, involve an inner process, and have an end, which is recognized as a realization of something that must be done. That is, there is a certain moral imperative regarding novenas, when crisis moments occur in the life of the individual or in the family or group.

A death in the family is an occasion for a novena. The nine days after the person dies is a time for the honorable completion of the duties of a Christian burial. The novena is just as important as having the Eucharist celebrated for the repose of the soul. It requires the presence of the members of the immediate and extended family, friends, and neighbors. From a human standpoint, the novena serves as a consoling event whereby the bereaved receive condolences beyond those customary at the time of the funeral; they are occasions for the spirit of bonding and fraternity to be expressed and reaffirmed.

The leader of the prayers of these novenas is not always an ordained minister. The usual case is that an acquaintance rises to the occasion. *La rezandera/rezandero*, the prayer leader, is invited to lead the rosary, which is followed by the Litany to the Blessed Virgin and other prayers for the dead.

There are other occasions for novenas, for example, the nine days immediately before a solemn feast. In Latin America and many places in North America, people gather before the feasts of Mary, under whatever title the nation has traditionally identified her (e.g., in Mexico, Our Lady of Guadalupe; in Cuba, *Nuestra Señora de la Caridad del Cobre*; in Puerto Rico, *Nuestra Señora de la Providencia*). The traditions are so ingrained that often the devotion of the novena prior to a solemn feast of Our Lady is celebrated in families regardless of whether they are celebrated in the parish church.

In Latin America, the Feast of the Nativity of Our Lord, December 25, is preceded by a novena of prayers and celebration called *Las Posadas*. A *posada* is a dwelling place for pilgrims; to give *posada* is to extend hospitality to those traveling, in particular strangers. The celebration of the *posada* reenacts the pilgrim journey of Mary and Joseph to Bethlehem and the search for a place where the Christ Child would be born. Statues of Mary and Joseph are carried from house to house; the journey is interspersed with the praying of the rosary, special hymns, and the Litany of the Blessed Virgin, often sung in its most solemn versions.

The *posada* celebration incorporates several Eucharistic themes. It is a communal event. In most barrios or neighborhoods, the time of *posadas* may be the only time families come together to do anything as a unit. The *posada* has a unique attraction that motivates people, young and old, rich and poor, to communion. There are the playful, dramatic, farcical, and festive moments that have something for everyone, and all this blended with the sacred reason for being together.

The family that plays host to the fiesta prepares for the event like no other during the rest of the year. The family that opens its doors to the people of the neighborhood is aware, even though the belief is not verbalized, that Jesus is coming into their home. The outward signs of the coming of Jesus are, of course, the pilgrim statues of Joseph and Mary, but also the sharing and hospitality extended by the host family. Seasonal sweets, and a hot, possibly spiced, fruit punch may be shared.

The children are led to the backyard or patio where they break the traditional piñata, a papier-mâché vessel in the shape of an animal, a star, or a comic book personage, filled with fruit, nuts, and candy. The piñata itself is symbolic of the attraction of sin and evil, particularly when the piñata has seven cones, representing the seven capital sins, attached to it; the stick with which the children hit it is God's grace. The person is blindfolded while attempting to hit the piñata, signifying the act of faith, which is accepting divine truths and promises without seeing. When the piñata is broken, the delicious contents drop out, representing the joys of heaven, the reward for a successful struggle between the forces of good and evil.

The elements of both novena and pilgrimage appear in the *posadas*. For nine days before Christmas, there is physical movement from one home to another. It involves a journeying, a reliving of the pilgrim experience of Mary and Joseph who are accompanied by fellow pilgrims in search of *la morada*, a place to rest and where comfort is found. The *posada* is a reenactment of the pilgrim experience of life itself. Life is a journey. In this life, Christians have no permanent habitat; that is reserved for the afterlife—the *mansion* that Jesus promised he would prepare. Like Augustine, the Christian pilgrim says, "We will not rest until we rest in Thee."

In the *posada* fiesta, the participants are reminded of their own transient state while in this world. However, we are not alone; as we march to our destiny, others who seek the same things the present state of being does not provide accompany us. Others inspire our determination, bring us out of our sometimes-sagging spirits, and drive us to take one more step; and we, too, are the source of inspiration for others. The pilgrimage state is a communal one, one of mutual need and assistance. The total experience is that of the *way*, which is living out the discipleship of Jesus.

A theme related to the Eucharist in the *posada* is the search. The pilgrims doing the *posada* associate themselves with Mary and Joseph in their search for a place of refuge. People in today's culture are continually searching for meaning, acceptance, security, and a way out of loneliness. The celebration of the Eucharist provides a place, most often the church, which like the home of the receiving family in the *posada*, is a place where some of these yearnings are fulfilled.

There is also a theme of the pilgrim as poor or needy. Our approach to Eucharist is as people in need; people, at the climax of worship, pray "Give us this day our daily bread"; people who know that all good things come from the provident God, referred to as the *Father*. Again, the association with Mary and Joseph brings pilgrims to experience themselves as *anawim*—the poor and lowly of the Old Testament, who find joy in Yahweh whom they recognize as their savior (Is. 29:19; Jer. 20: 13).[4] The pilgrim of the *posada* experiences rejection and the closing of doors. The emphasis on prayer between homes is a reminder that when human recourse is not possible, all things are possible with God. He will deliver us from want and obtain for us the total liberation that we seek.

---

[4] Albert Gelin, *The Poor of Yahweh* (Collegeville, MN: Liturgical Press, 1964).

Another Eucharistic theme is the practice of hospitality. At least at this time of the year, a family plays host to neighbors. The family sometimes even welcomes strangers, and the occasion is the visit to the family of the guest of honor, the parents of the Christ Child and Jesus himself. It is a reminder of the enthronement of Christ at the Ascension and the end-time of the *parusía*. The door, the front door, is open, symbolic as if it were the doors of the hearts opening to receive the life of Jesus. The invitation to all to enter is a sign of absence of prejudice and suspicion; it is a sign of reconciliation and peace among friends.

A festive element of *posada* ties to the Eucharist. The *posada* is an example of the realization of one of the ideals of Eucharist—a true celebration with its festive qualities: loss of the sense of time; a joyful event made complete by the presence of friends; the absence of an ulterior motive for fiesta, other than the religious–human one of Jesus incarnated as one of us. Indeed fiesta is the sign of the Kingdom promised by Jesus, the Kingdom whereby justice is for all and peace is possible. Fiesta is the celebration of fraternity and unity; all enjoy the same bread and wine, sing the same songs, dance to the same rhythm, and share the best of life—the good times that make everything in life worthwhile. God, who is present through Jesus, Mary, and Joseph, sanctions all this. This is God's celebration, too, for it reveals the reality of His dream that His children be one, that they share their goods, that in this way justice be experienced. In a fleeting moment, *la posada* is expressive of the two dreams becoming one: that of God and that of humankind. Both share the same aspiration for His creation: freedom, unity, and love.

Chapter 9

Mary at the Threshold of the New Creation

It was a cold night in South Texas; a blue norther had just come through and cleared the sky. In the cool crispness of that evening, we walked a few yards from the home of my grandparents, where my immediate family lived, to the home of Tía Petra and her family. At four years old, I did not know why we were going to Tía Petra's; after supper, we usually did not do much, especially in the winter when it was uncomfortable to leave the house.

That night, family and neighbors gathered to begin the novena to Our Lady of Guadalupe. I found out later this was the yearly custom of the extended family. I had probably seen the altarcito in the corner of the main room of Tía Petra's house before, but never paid too much attention to it. This time, a couple of candles were lit in front of Our Lady's image, and I still remember the pictures of the four apparitions at each corner. I also remember my Tía Petra, a woman whom I had only seen in her role as tortilla maker, clothes washer, lunch maker, and general mujer de la casa (woman of the house). She was a woman with a ready smile and always had a word of encouragement.

That evening, she took out a black book, obviously old, with its tattered, yellow-aged pages that kept falling out. She took out an *equally worn rosary and began speaking to the picture at an unbelievable speed. She broke all prayer speed limits! The whole scene entranced me; I would first look at the image with the flickering candles before it, then look at my family, with their eyes either intent on what they were saying or on the image of Our Lady of Guadalupe. I do not remember just how long the scene captivated me, but I do remember very vividly what happened next.*

As we were walking back to our grandparents' home that cold, dark night, I took my grandfather's hand and, after walking a few paces with him, he reached down, and for no explainable reason, except for his cariño *(love) for me, he lifted me up and sat me on his shoulders. I looked up and saw a million stars set against the black sky. It was at that moment that I sensed a special presence of the someone who made those stars, and in childlike fashion, I surmised that all of those stars had been made for me. I remember saying to myself, "Whoever you are, who made all these stars for me, thank you!"*

It was in that context of devotion to Guadalupe, family intimacy, and the sense of grandeur that God started reaching out and initiating a lifelong familiarity with me. I sincerely believe that my Christian vocation began at that very precise moment—and all in the milieu created by Tía Petra's novena.

* * *

As I reflect on Tía Petra's novena, I am sure that it was there that I discovered the world of the sacred. This happened at the hearing of new and sacred utterances (my Tía Petra's rapid rattling of prayers with the rest of the family responding). I saw objects then that I had never noticed before, such as the image of Our Lady of Guadalupe flanked by two candles, the rosary, and my Tía's tattered prayer book. The different bodily postures and facial expressions of my family further impressed me. It was not every day that my family knelt together to utter sacred sounds. I was sure that something very special and extraordinary was going on, something that had to do with everything else. I could not explain it then, but now I know that it was a mountaintop encounter with the invisible God by way of His visible mother.

On a corner shelf of Tía Petra's humble home was a print of the image of Our Lady of Guadalupe. This print was probably my first glimpse of her image. Throughout the rest of my life, I would gaze on this image thousands of times. She is everywhere in the Latino world; it is a frequent subject of Latino art; it is seen in people's homes, in our churches, on murals, on human bodies as tattoos, on holy cards, and on vehicles, especially low-riders. It is worn as medals around people's necks and on bracelets.

After the papal Mass at the Basilica of Our Lady of Guadalupe on February 13, 2016, Pope Francis was given the opportunity to sit up close to the image; he prayed in silence for twenty-five minutes while the massive crowds inside and outside the basilica observed a respectful silence.

What was unique about Tía Petra's image was that at each corner of the print there was a picture of one of the apparitions to the Indian, now a saint, Juan Diego. Those pictures were the visual representation of the story found in the *Nican Mopohua* ("Thus it is told").

The Apparitions

In the beautiful poetic elements of the Nahuatl language, even in the English and Spanish translations, the words are stunningly attractive. According to the *Nican Mopohua,* the Lady first appeared to Juan Diego on December 9, 1531, as he was walking to early Mass at the church at Tlatelolco. In the midst of beautiful music, he heard a voice calling him, "*Juanito, Juan Dieguito.*" On top of the hill of Tepeyac, he saw the Virgin clothed with the sun, with a face of love and compassion. She asked him where he was going, and he answered that he was going to be taught about divine things. Right away she introduced herself as the "Holy Virgin Mary, Mother of the True God through whom one lives, mother of the creator of heaven and of earth." She asked him to go to the bishop and ask that a temple be built on the hill of Tepeyac. There, in that temple, she said she would show her love, compassion, help, and defense. There she would hear their lamentations and remedy their miseries, pains, and sufferings.

Juan Diego went quickly to the bishop's palace, and after a long wait, he gave the bishop the message of the Lady. Even though the bishop was kind, he told him to come another day. Juan Diego felt he had failed in his mission.

The second apparition happened again on Tepeyac. He explained to the dear Lady what had happened and that the bishop did not seem to have time for him. He begged her to entrust her mission to an important person who was well known, respected, and esteemed. He said of himself, "I am nobody, a nothing, a coward, a pile of old sticks, just a bunch of leaves." The Lady told him that she still wanted him to return to the bishop. Juan Diego accepted her mandate and said he would return to the bishop but that he was not very hopeful.

In his second visit to the bishop, he answered the bishop's many questions. The bishop was unbelieving and said that he needed some sign.

In the third apparition, Juan Diego reported to the Virgin that the bishop wanted a sign. She agreed to this and said that the next day she would have the sign the bishop requested and that he, Juan Diego, would be rewarded.

When he arrived at home, he discovered that his uncle Juan Bernardino was gravely ill, and Juan Diego spent the rest of the day searching for medical help. He was not able to find anyone, but he promised his uncle that the next morning he would go to Tlatelolco to have a priest confess him and prepare him for death.

The morning of Tuesday, December 12, 1531, on his way to Tlatelolco and fearing that the Lady might detain him, he took a different route, but the Lady found him anyway. Juan Diego explained about his uncle and that as soon as he could take care of getting him a priest, he would return to the Lady.

She told him not to be troubled and assured him that his uncle would not die, and she told him to go to the top of the hill where he would find various flowers. She told him to cut and gather the flowers and bring them to her. At the top, he was astounded to discover many beautiful roses of Castille, and this was in the middle of winter. He cut them and returned to the Lady with the roses. She took them into her hands and rearranged them in his *tilma*, the cactus fiber cloak that he was wearing. She asked him to take the roses to the bishop.

Full of joy, he hurried to the house of the bishop, for he knew that this time the bishop would believe him. Once more, he described to the bishop all that he had seen and the message of the Lady to have a temple built on Tepeyac hill. He explained about the beautiful roses, the sign sent by the Lady. As he unfolded his *tilma,* the roses dropped to the floor. But it was not the roses that impressed the bishop and his attendants. It was the image of the Holy Virgin Mary impressed on Juan Diego's *tilma*. All fell to their knees and believed.

A Reflection on Tía Petra's Novena

The following theological themes and concepts regarding God and the act of faith were all very much present at Tía Petra's novena.

God reveals Himself. This is the basic principle of the revelation of God as described in Vatican II's Dogmatic Constitution on Divine Revelation, *Dei Verbum*: "It pleased God, in His goodness and wisdom, to reveal Himself and to make known the mystery of His will" (cf. Eph. 1:9).

The God of Jesus is the God of love. He loves from afar, but He is also very much present. In other words, our belief is in a transcendent and immanent God. In the Old Testament, God is so near that in His theophanies, he actually speaks directly to patriarchs, prophets, and kings. In the New Testament, the Risen Lord wants to assure His disciples of His protective nearness. "Do not fear, it is I" (Matt. 14:27). In both Old and New Testaments, the ambivalence of transcendence/immanence recurs repeatedly. At the call of Moses, the Lord is so close that the two talk to each other, but at the same time, the Lord maintains His distance: "Come no nearer! Remove the sandals from your feet, for the place where you stand is holy ground" (Exod. 3:4–5). At the transfiguration, Jesus is transformed totally and becomes totally other in an awe-inspiring manner—yet there is a familiarity created, and Peter is prompted to say, "Lord, how good that we are here! With your permission, I will erect three booths here, one for you, one for Moses, and one for Elijah" (Matt. 17:4).

The story of Our Lady of Guadalupe also reflects the transcendence/immanence of divine revelation. Our Lady speaks tenderly and lovingly to the Indian Juan Diego. They carry on some beautiful conversations together. Yet when one examines the image left on Juan's *tilma*, one notices that, while the face is that of a beautiful lady, there are other signs that reflect that she is from somewhere beyond, and not of this world. The *tilma* shows Guadalupe dressed in a mantle filled with stars; her dress is richly decorated; the sun is behind her back; and there is a black moon under her feet.

Another theological element that was present at Tía Petra's novena was the way in which the act of faith occurred. The beginning of the process of faith is always through the mediation of someone else. We believe because others believe. Faith is therefore *caught* by way of the witness of those close to us. Furthermore, the act of faith involves a whole person: psychologically, emotionally, and intellectually. It was the witness of Tía Petra, family, and neighbors, in the event described above, that brought God to me and me to God.

Mary in Sacred Scripture

Reflecting on Tía Petra's novena and my own act of faith, I see a parallel in the Scriptures with Abraham and the promise of a progeny that would *number the stars*. Abraham and I have something in common; we both experienced the transcendent God as we beheld the cosmos.

I also see a parallel between my first act of faith and Moses and the burning bush. My burning bush was the scene of my extended family gathered around the candle-lit image of the Virgin of Guadalupe. Like Moses, I was surprised by what was happening and, at the same time, captivated. The God of Moses was the God of Tía Petra.

I really believe that my vocation to the Christian life and to the priesthood came that night. The experience has parallels in the *anawim*, the little people in the history of salvation.[1] God's

---

[1] Albert Gelin, *The Poor of Yahweh* (Collegeville, MN: Liturgical Press, 1964).

revelation and purpose so often happen in the Scriptures by way of the young, the humble, and the poor, such as David, Saul, Samuel, Isaiah, Elizabeth, Joseph, Simeon, and Anna, to name but a few. I am now the bishop emeritus of Las Cruces, and have been a bishop for thirty-five years, but back then I was a three- or four-year-old child of a poor family.

I am sure there have been times in my life that I had fearful images of God, but I have never really failed to believe that the God who is and will be forever is a loving one—such as described in John 3:16: "God so loved the world that he sent His only Son."

The Scriptures often relate the mystery of vocation in both the Old and New Testaments. We do not know exactly why God chose the Jews or why He chose Abraham, Moses, or Jacob. At the moment of initial vocation, there is no reason why the prophets were chosen; some of them admitted their ignorance and their unworthiness. The same thing happens in the New Testament with Peter who stumbles around, with Philip who questions everything, and with Thomas who doubts it all. Paul admittedly relates his own wrestling with his calling, since he did not witness the resurrection at the historical moment in which it occurred. Those of us who have been called to the priesthood often question, "Why me?" and in my case, "Why did God choose me, when there are so many others with far greater intellectual, spiritual, and human capacities?" That is the mystery of vocation.

In the Scriptures, particularly in Luke and John, Mary occupies a unique place in the history of salvation. Her presence in the Scriptures never takes away from her Son Jesus Christ. He is always the star or the sun, and she the moon, reflecting only the light that she receives from her Son. John places the mother of Jesus at the beginning of his earthly mission at the wedding feast of Cana. She later appears in

John only at the end of the Gospel, at the foot of the cross. The Mother of Jesus in John seems to provide the framework for the entire Gospel. While she is not mentioned in the in-between chapters, by placing the Mother of Jesus at the beginning and at the end, she seems to be nonetheless always present, but in the background. In my own spiritual journey, the Mother of Jesus has always been there, caring, nurturing, understanding, and oftentimes simply listening.

Mary at the Threshold of the New Evangelization

From the perspective of the New Evangelization proposed by St. John Paul II for the third millennium, focus on Mary under the title of *Santa María de Guadalupe* is most appropriate (the origin of the name *Guadalupe* is actually Arabic). The early missionaries had come from the area of Extremadura in Spain where a small wooden image was venerated under the title of *Nuestra Señora de Guadalupe*. The name itself comes from two Arabic words, *guadi* and *lupus*, meaning the *hidden river*. The River Guadalupe is indeed hidden in a deep ravine. One can hear it, but one cannot see it from its high banks. Parallel roles of Mary as instrument of God's plan can be noted from both sacred Scripture and from the history of the first evangelization of America. This moment, as we begin the third millennium of Christianity, is an opportune time to refer to her as the Mother of the New Creation for she stands in scriptural tradition as well as in history "at the threshold."

The reference to Mary as the Mother of the New Creation[2] has a basis in the Scriptures. We recall the wedding

[2] Virgil Elizondo, *Guadalupe: Mother of the New Creation* (Maryknoll, NY: Orbis Books, 1997).

feast at Cana, when Jesus calls Mary "woman," he is, in the tradition of John the Evangelist, calling her the new Eve, who appears at the threshold of the new creation and a key figure in the beginning of the "book of signs" (1:19–12:50). There she is helping inaugurate her son's ministry, his road to glory and that of the world, which he has come to save. In John, Mary is the privileged first hearer of the *hour* of the new exodus, the Passover, the death to resurrection for the life of the world.

At Calvary, she is there, as if to complete the frame of her son's ministry. As she had been there at the inauguration, she is now present at the culmination: *stabat mater dolorosa*, at the moment of the end that we know is only the beginning.

In the Lucan tradition, Mary is at various thresholds. There is first the threshold of the annunciation, where she learns of her role in the divine plan to save the world. There her *yes*, her acceptance of her role, is the answer given in the name of all believers and in the name of the world. She echoes the many yesses of her ancestors, beginning with the patriarchs, Abraham, Isaac, Jacob, Moses; the prophets; the kings; and all the saints of the Old Covenant. Being at the threshold, she is also prefiguring the *yes* of the new, of those to come, of the saints, washed in the blood of the lamb.

Her stand at the threshold becomes clearer at the visitation to Elizabeth. There in her song of salvific joy, the *Magnificat*, she speaks as the corporate personality of both the people of God of the old dispensation and the people of God of the new.

We could also see her at the threshold of Jesus's earthly life and ministry at his birth and at the moment of finding him in the temple. At these two occasions, similar expressions are given: "Mary treasured all these things and reflected on them in her heart" (Luke 2:19), and "His mother kept all these things in memory" (Luke 2:51).

Given the prominence Luke gives Mary at the threshold of salvation, we are not surprised to find her at the beginning of new forms of her son's presence in the world through the Holy Spirit. She is the one who, after the Ascension, seems to keep the faith of the apostles alive and leads them in praying for the coming of the fire, the wind, and the breath that is the life of the new creation.

The Virgin of Guadalupe Appears

Thus far, I have reflected on Mary of Nazareth. I turn now to Mary of Tepeyac, *la Virgen de Guadalupe*, where again she is at the threshold of the first evangelization of America. The apostolic exhortation of St. John Paul II, *Ecclesia in America*, makes significant references to Guadalupe. He reminds us of her special role in the Christianization of these lands. "From the beginning—invoked as Our Lady of Guadalupe—Mary, by her motherly and merciful figure, was a great sign of the closeness of the Father and of Jesus Christ, with whom she invites us to enter into communion" (no. 11).

St. John Paul II made note of the 1531 appearance and her influence beyond the boundaries of Mexico. Because she is the first to announce Jesus Christ in the hemisphere and because of her pedagogy, she is aptly designated the "Star of the evangelization" of America.

The Virgin of Guadalupe visits Mexico in its most agonizing moment. The Spaniards arrived in 1519 on the shores of Mexico in the area where the city of Veracruz now stands. The Aztecs thought that the promised return of one of their heroes, Quetzalcoatl, had arrived and were joyful at first. A short time later, the painful conquest began. The coming together of the Europeans and the Indians of America was not a pleasant encounter; quite the contrary, it was a clash of cultures, a clash of two cosmic visions, and a clash of theologies. Powerful poetry was composed by the Aztecs, especially by those who experienced the battles in Tenochtitlan, now Mexico City, and its neighboring suburb, Talatelolco. The conquest happened in the midst of death, destruction, pillage, rape, and disease. Millions throughout the Americas died because of smallpox, to which the Indians had no biological defense. The following is a poem of lament written at the time.[3]

> Broken spears lie in the roads
> We have torn our hair in our grief
> The houses are roofless now, and their walls
> Are red with blood.
> Worms are swarming in the streets and plazas,
> And the walks are spattered with gore
> The water has turned red, as if it were dyed
> And when we drink it,
> It has the taste of brine
> We have pounded our hands in despair
> Against the adobe walls,
> For our inheritance, our city, is lost and dead
> The shields of our warriors were its defense.
> But they could not save it.

The Virgin of Guadalupe appeared as a symbol of peace; over time, she became a bridge between peoples in the midst of pain, death, and sorrow. For the Indian she was *Tonantzin*, the mother of the gods; for the European she was the Mother of Jesus. She was acceptable to both. To make an introduction, to present one person to another, one must know both. In the case of Guadalupe, she knows her son as no one had or

---

[3] Miguel León-Portilla, *The Broken Spears: The Aztec Account of the Conquest of Mexico* (Boston: Beacon Press, 2006), 135.

has ever known him. However, she also knows, through the person of Juan Diego, the peoples of the land we now know as America. She knows the anguished state of the vanquished Indian; she understands well his plight; she knows the coming together of the peoples of Europe and the New World is not happening harmoniously, but rather in the context of bloodshed and horrible violence to a people and its cultural wealth.

She understands her new children, the way they perceive themselves and the world in which they have their being, and she knows how best to approach them to elicit the response of faith and love. This wisdom makes her such a successful evangelizer. Mary is the first ambassador of Jesus Christ at the threshold of the first evangelization and at the dawn of the coming together of different races, languages, and cultures.

Her face is that of a *mestizo*, the new race being born at the time of Spanish and Indian blood. The first *mestizo* children were unacceptable to the Indians and the Spaniards. Indian women did not always love their *mestizo* children, and many of them were aborted or killed at birth. Likewise, the Spaniards could not accept these children because they were not of their race. The face of Our Lady of Guadalupe is that of a *mestiza*, as if to say, "It is all right to be who you are, for I am one of you." She gives legitimacy to those thought of as illegitimate. Beyond this acceptance lie love, care, and mercy.

St. John Paul II in *Ecclesia in America* refers to her *mestizo* face when he refers to America as the "melting pot" (in Spanish, *crisol*, or crucible), and where she is referred to as the impressive example of a perfectly enculturated evangelization (no. 11). The face of Guadalupe expresses compassion and understanding, and to the Indian she manifests the maternal, the tender side of God.

The image of Guadalupe and her message are beautiful examples of the enculturation of the Gospel. The missionaries in the sixteenth century in the New World belittled and condemned the culture, which they perceived as base and demonic; they set out to destroy the indigenous culture, and their aim was to Europeanize the Indians in order that they become Christianized. Guadalupe does not ignore the presence of God already as *seeds of the Word* that were preparing the ground for the truth of the Gospel. She does not put aside the Gospel vision of the Indian; rather she assumes it, recognizes it, and uses it to teach about the one true God of Jesus Christ. As an eminent pastoral theologian, Segundo Galilea, puts it, "Mary of Guadalupe drank of the well belonging to the host *Náhuatl* culture."

The written account of the apparitions is found in the poetic masterpiece, the *Nican Mopohua*. The *Nican Mopohua* was written in *Náhuatl*, the Aztec language—still the indigenous language most spoken in Mexico today. Almost every verse expresses in mythic–symbolic language the philosophical, theological, and anthropological world of the *Náhuatl* people—among the first in the New World to be evangelized. It incorporates linguistic and symbolic concepts regarding the indigenous understanding of the cosmic order. Guadalupe enters the world of Juan Diego accompanied by the songs of birds. "He heard singing on the summit of the hill: as if different precious birds were singing and their songs would alternate, as if the hill was answering them. Their song was most pleasing and enjoyable, better than the *coyoltótol* or of the *tzinizcan* or of the other precious birds that sing."[4]

Flowers adorn the divine encounter between the Indian, Juan Diego, and the Virgin. Flowers become the symbolic proof not only for the Bishop Juan Zumárraga but also for the people themselves. "All over the place there were all kinds of exquisite flowers from Castile, open and flowering. It was

---

[4] "*La Evangelización Guadalupana,*" *Estudios Indígenas* 7, no. 2 (March 1981): 189.

not a place for flowers, and likewise it was the time when the ice hardens upon the earth."

Flower and song, *flor y canto*, were enough for the observant *Náhuatl* eyes and ears to understand, in the most profound recesses of the mind and heart, that this was a divine revelation. In the eloquent words of Fr. Virgil Elizondo,

> Rational discourse clarifies yet limits the mind, while flowers and song stimulate the imagination to ponder the infinite. For the *Náhuatl*, it was only through poetic communication and beauty that the heart of human beings could enter into communion and communication with the divine. For the *Náhuatl*, truth was expressed through the suggestive harmony of the seen and heard. Through the beauty of the image (flowers) and the melodious sounds (poetic word), the divine could be gradually experienced, and one could gradually come to share in divine wisdom.[5]

The following poem in the words of the Aztec people describes the approach to the divine in flower and song:

> I look for you oh Father God, giver of life
> I look for you in the sweetness of your flowers
> The joy of your songs, your richness!
> And again:
> Oh priest, I ask you, where do those flowers come from?
> The song that enthralls me, that beautiful song?
> They come solely from your home,
> From the inner heavens,
> Solely from there do the many flowers have their origin.[6]

---

[5] Elizondo, *Guadalupe,* 35.
[6] Unknown Aztec poet.

The exclamation of the Indian, San Juan Diego, reflects the approach to the divine in flower and song. As he reached the base of the hill known as Tepeyac at daybreak, he heard singing atop the hill, resembling the singing of various beautiful birds. Juan Diego stopped and said to himself, "By fortune, am I worthy of what I hear? Maybe I dream. Am I awakening? Where am I? Our elders told us about the terrestrial paradise. Is this it? Perhaps I am in heaven." Later in the story, "Immediately Juan Diego climbed the hill, and as he reached the summit, he was amazed to see so many varieties of exquisite *rosas de Castilla* were blooming, long before the time when they are to bud, because, being out of season, they would freeze. They were fragrant and covered with dewdrops of the night, which resembled precious pearls."

The most striking symbol on the miraculous image is that of a *Náhuatl* glyph, placed directly at the center, over the womb of the Virgin. The glyph is in the form of a four-petal flower, which could also be the formation of a cross. For the indigenous peoples in many parts of the Americas, the number four is part of their *cosmovisión* (worldview). In New Mexico, for example, the Navajo Indians revere the symbol of the *"zía,"* and it is at the center of the state flag. The *zía* is four sets of rays shooting out of a circle. The circle represents peace and harmony. The four rays, of four lines each, represent the four ideals: a sound body, a sound mind, a generous heart, and service to the community.

The indigenous eye would immediately associate the glyph on the image of Our Lady of Guadalupe with the Aztec representation of the cosmos as seen in the Aztec calendar, now the crowning piece of the National Museum of Anthropology in Mexico City. The *Náhuatl* interpretation of this symbol was that a new age was arriving with this latest of *suns*, the fifth one. The placement of this symbol over her womb indicates that she carries within herself the new source and center of the humanity of the final age. "As in the incarnation God chose to begin through the cooperation of a woman, so now, too, the coming together of the entire planet for the first time will begin with a woman."[7] That source and center is the living Jesus Christ, and his mother makes the introduction to the peoples of America in a perfectly crafted pedagogy.

The bishops at the Synod for America and St. John Paul II saw in Guadalupe a most appropriate symbol for the new evangelization. At this special moment in the history of the church, she again occupies her place at the threshold. The Virgin of Guadalupe is more than a symbol of the new evangelization. Her image and her story offer an example of evangelization at its best, for they communicate clearly and powerfully the coming of the God of Jesus Christ into the world of the indigenous peoples.

She wants to make sure Juan Diego understands who she is and whom she represents. She says, "I am the ever Virgin Mary, mother of the true God [*Teotl Dios Inantzin*], for whom we live, [*Ipalnemohuani*], the creator of all things [*Teyocoyani*], and mother of heaven and earth [*Ilhuicahua Tlaltipaque*]." These were the different names given to the Aztec belief in their one god, *Ometeotl*, the god of duality, who incorporated in his person those mysterious opposites as life and death, light and darkness, good and evil.

Another indication of her masterful evangelization is the design on the rose-colored dress. The design is a representation of the *amaranto* plant and seed, or amaranth in English. The Indian eye would perceive that she brings spiritual nutrition, healing, and sweetness, for the *amaranto* was part of their staple diet and was full of rich elements. The amaranth tea was medicinal, so the Virgin was bringing healing. The Indians would fashion little idols with the amaranth and honey. They

---

[7] Elizondo, *Guadalupe,* 128.

would then eat these idols, and it was in that way that they were in communion with their god.

Guadalupe:
The Symbol for the New Creation

Just as Guadalupe became the symbol in America for the encounter with the living Jesus Christ in the sixteenth century, so in the task toward the new creation in the next millennium, she becomes the symbol for the new encounter, the new conversion, the new communion, and the new solidarity—the civilization of love. As a symbol, she points to what is already and to what is yet to be achieved. We are one in faith, united by the spirit of the living God and around the table of the Eucharist, but the ideal of the solidarity, about which the Holy Father speaks in *Ecclesia in America*, is far from being a reality.

As a dominant and primordial symbol, she serves as a reminder of various things. She reminds us of the maternal and tender love of the eternal God. She reminds us of the loving embrace of the Christian faith by those gone before us, beginning with the sixteenth century, and that we are heirs to a superabundant spiritual tradition. The image of Guadalupe tells us that in spite of radical differences of race, cultures, and economic levels, it is possible to be one human family, civilized in love and characterized by an enduring spirit and reality of solidarity. She reminds us, first of all, of the mandate and highest aspiration of Jesus in his priestly prayer that *we be one*. She reminds us that we believers enjoy the supernatural gift of *comunio*, and she is here among us to strengthen our faith and our unity in the living Christ, who leads us to the Father with the power of the Holy Spirit.

She is a reminder that through tragedy and jubilation, her and her son accompany us. We have not been abandoned, as she promised at Guadalupe. I am convinced when Tía Petra brought us together to pray the Novena to Our Lady of Guadalupe, it was out of thanksgiving for her accompaniment of my family's journey from Mexico to the United States and for having been an inspiration along the way.

The Virgin of Guadalupe reminds us of the priority and solidarity we must give the poor and the marginalized, understood in America as the indigenous and people of African origin, of the unemployed and underemployed, of exploited women and children, the rejected immigrant, the incarcerated, the elderly, and all with whom Jesus identifies himself.

The Virgin of Guadalupe chooses to go to the margins, to the little people, the forgotten, and the ignored. When San Juan Diego reports to the Virgin that the bishop would not see him, he asks that she send someone else. He says, "Someone of importance, well-known and esteemed, so that they may believe in him, because I am a nobody, I am a small rope, a tiny ladder, the tail-end, a leaf, and you, my child, the least of my children, my Lady, you send me to a place where I never visit nor repose."

To these remarks, the Virgin replies, "Hark my son, the least, you must understand is that I have many servants and messengers to whom I must entrust the delivery of my message, and carry my wish, but it is of precise detail that you yourself solicit and assist, and that through your mediation my wish be complied."

The Virgin thus speaks to San Juan Diego, who represents the undervalued, those not readily noticed, the belittled in every way. By encouraging the Indian and motivating him, she is encouraging all peoples to recognize their value. The temple that she wishes erected in her honor is for all people, men and women, of every race and culture, that they can come and seek her intercession; and yet all she offers is her tender and merciful face. She encourages them to be builders of their own destiny for she, by her presence and words, transforms them from the lifelessness of oppression to lives of self-worth, confidence, and a sense of belonging. When we visit the Shrine of Our Lady of Guadalupe, we come away with the impression that people, in fact, do receive new courage and strength to continue striving for lives that reflect their dignity and importance.

God, through Guadalupe, also gives us hope. As Pope Francis said in his homily at the Shrine of Our Lady of Guadalupe on February 13, 2016,

> On that morning, God roused the hope of the little ones, of the suffering, of those displaced or rejected, of all who feel they have no worthy place in these lands. On that morning, God came close and still comes close to the suffering but resilient hearts of so many mothers, fathers, grandparents who have seen their children leaving, becoming lost or even being taken by criminals.

Her beautiful dark countenance inspires us to look toward the coming millennium with hope and confidence. "*¡Sí se puede!*" she says to us.

This is the message Latinos in the United States need to listen to over and over again, especially those truly at the margins because of their poverty, immigration status, discrimination, and whose culture is ridiculed and devalued. Young Latinos especially need to recognize their value and potential as Latinos embracing their rich cultural heritage.

Chapter 10

------◆·◆·◆------

Worship as Fiesta

Just outside of Las Cruces is an Indian village popularly known as Tortugas but whose official name is Mesilla Park, New Mexico. For well over one hundred years, the Indians have been celebrating the Feast of Our Lady of Guadalupe in a unique and spiritual way. I was privileged to lead parts of this fiesta for all but two of the years I was the bishop of Las Cruces.

Days ahead of the feast, the people of the village go out into the desert and gather dried yucca stems that will be decorated and used as walking sticks during the traditional rituals.

On the eve of December 12, that is, December 11, there is the annual trek up Tortugas Mountain about four or five miles from the village. The pilgrimage begins early in the morning around 7 a.m., and people start walking across the desert, crossing two major interstate highways on their way.

The physical hardship begins at the base of Tortugas Mountain, which takes a good hour to climb. While it is not a long trip up, it is extremely steep and somewhat dangerous because of the loose rocks and sharp cactus thorns.

At the top of the mountain, there will be hundreds of people eagerly awaiting the celebration of the Eucharist. People line up in front of the various priests who hear their confessions.

The Mass takes place usually under severe winter weather conditions, and it sometimes snows during the Mass. One year it rained so hard that I celebrated the fastest Mass in the West.

After a festive Mass, people gather around campfires, where they warm tamales, burritos, and coffee to be shared by those who may not have brought anything to eat.

There are sounds of laughter, children squealing, and the crackling of burning coals. The aromas of burning mesquite and creosote bushes, the incense from the single sacred fire, and charred tortillas filled with beans and chile fill the air. Nothing is sold, and there is no glaring popular music. Liquor is absent, and there is nothing but the joy of sharing in honor of la Virgen. A rosary is recited during the afternoon.

Toward sunset, a signal is given from the village church that they may descend the mountain and bring their yucca sticks, called quiotes, which the people have decorated, to offer to the Virgin in lieu of roses. When they arrive in the village, they go to a small chapel where the image of Our Lady of Guadalupe is enthroned. They knock on the door three times before the door is finally opened. Those three knocks are symbolic of St. Juan Diego going to Bishop Juan Zumárraga, the bishop of Mexico City in 1531, when the apparitions of Our Lady of Guadalupe took place. When the doors of the chapel open, people process in singing hymns to Mary and depositing quiotes at her simple shrine. Then the Indian ritual dances begin. They dance late into the night.

The next morning, people come into the parish church to celebrate Mass, which is usually presided over by the bishop. Half of the church is occupied by the Indian dancers, and these are usually young people. Afterward the various Indian groups dance in front and on the sides of the parish church. The preeminent group is the one sponsored by the Corporation of the Indians; they own the property around the church.

Young boys, accompanied by their aunts, play central roles in the dance, which is performed to the cadence of Indian drums and ancient chants. At a given moment, rifles are fired into the air, and people begin to process toward the Casa de Comida for the annual festive community meal. Before entering the dining hall, all of the people, including the bishop and priests, form a huge circle and perform a simple dance as an act of thanksgiving. After the blessing before the meal, large bowls and platters of food are brought in, and the menu is always the same: chile colorado, frijoles, albóndigas, macaroni with cheese, coffee, and hot chocolate. As they leave the dining hall, all are offered biscochitos (Mexican fiesta cookies) and other sweets. The dancing continues during the day.

*   *   *

The annual fiesta in honor of Our Lady of Guadalupe in the village of Tortugas incorporates so many elements: music, dance, colorful costumes, tradition, food, pilgrimage, community, and above all the Eucharist. This fiesta is unique; it is distinctive from any other fiestas, including those I experienced in Mexico. One of the reasons is that it centers on the Eucharist. In many ways, the festivities lead to, and celebrate, the Eucharist; and the Eucharist is an essential part of the overall experience. Other Eucharistic elements are present, particularly the inclusion of everyone, since all are welcome. There is a certain purity about this celebration; there is nothing commercial about it, and nothing is for sale. While there is great importance placed on the Blessed Virgin, Mary of Guadalupe, the Eucharist makes the celebration Christ-centered.

When we enter the world of ritual and symbol, we take time from our ordinary lives and enter sacred space and time. For example, the feast days of Our Lady of Guadalupe do not usually fall on a weekend, which makes it necessary for the participants to ask to be excused from work or school. Neither do we approach God in worship with empty hands. We bring the substance of our lives to the altar and then, after the Eucharist, we take to our lives the memory of Jesus, his message, and the way of life, He wants us to follow. There is a vital connection between what we do in worship and how we live our lives.

Going up the mountain in honor of Our Lady of Guadalupe and celebrating Eucharist at the top reminds us that the Eucharist is central to our Christian lives and that it is the source and summit of everything we do as disciples of Jesus.

Why Empty Pews?

So many people who call themselves Catholic Christians do not go to Mass. The Pew Research Center reports that during the past four decades "self-reported church attendance has declined. The share of all Catholics who say they attend Mass at least once a week has dropped from 47% in 1974 to 24% in 2012." Among those absent from Eucharist are probably many Latinos who claim to be Catholics.

While many thousands of Latinos lined the streets of the US cities that Pope Francis visited, Latinos did not flock in great numbers to return to the church after his visit. What is more than likely true is that practicing Latino Catholics have become more serious and more devout because of Pope Francis's visit to the United States.

I was once vacationing in New York City, and I was there on a Sunday morning. I decided I would attend Mass as a congregant and not ask to concelebrate. The Mass was on the boring side, and the homily was so-so. Of course, the rubrics of the Roman Mass were faithfully observed. After communion, a Latino woman got up to make the announcements.

Her excited voice, her hand gestures, and her humor made the entire congregation come alive. In fact, even though she was only announcing events to take place later that week in the parish, it was the most exciting part of the Mass. It made me think that there is so much life in the Latino world and what a challenge we have to bring that Latino spirit into worship. It is no wonder that people leave the Catholic Church, with its emphasis on rubrics, and resort to more enlivened prayer and song in the evangelical churches.

I observed the elaborate Masses held in the various Latin American countries that Pope Francis visited in the summer of 2015. On Pope Francis's way to the sites where he was to lead the Mass, the streets and highways were lined with hundreds of thousands of joyful and excited people waving and cheering the pope. Once the Mass started, the pope was greeted with sacred songs appropriate to the cultures of the people he was leading in prayer. The musical compositions honored the Latin American rhythms and melodies, and the choirs were mostly successful in leading the rest of the people in singing.

It happened at the Masses in Cuba, which the pope visited on his way to the United States. The music honored the Caribbean style of blended rhythms that inspired people to clap and move with the music. The disconnect, however, was the actual liturgy itself as it unfolded around the altar. The festive spirit of the people lined along the streets as the pope went by and the inspired music ended when the Mass began. The Masses were Roman and very dead. While the rubrics were followed faithfully, the Masses lacked the expression of the high moment of joy among the people. Even the pope was serious and unsmiling during the ritual of the Mass.

More recently, the Eucharistic celebrations during the pope's visit to Mexico were more in keeping with local culture. I was moved deeply by the Mass in San Cristobal de

Las Casas, Chiapas. We witnessed a successful incorporation of the beauty of the Mayan cultures of the region into the liturgy. The art and environment were a blend of indigenous color and folk art. The backdrop was a replica of the façade of the Cathedral of San Cristobal. Native instruments, such as the marimba, accompanied the music. Three Mayan languages, Tzotzil, Tzeltal, and Chol, were used. The people also celebrated during the Mass with regional dances.

Unfortunately, the liturgy in the local parish shows a greater disconnect with Latin cultures. We proclaim the Gospel of Joy at Mass. Yet, where is the joy we proclaimed? The only time I see people smiling is when they give the sign of peace to one another.

It is true, however, that not all people bring joy every time they go to Mass. As children, we learned a silly song accompanied by an equally silly movement. We would form a circle, holding hands, and we would move around to the song:

A la rueda, la rueda de San Miguel, todos traen su caja de miel.

A lo maduro, a lo maduro, que se voltee Ricardo de burro!

Translated, this means, "To the circle of St. Michael, all bring a box of honey. When the time comes, let Ricardo turn into a burro." When my name was called, I would turn around and keep holding hands with those next to me until all were turned backward after their names were called. That was it. It was a silly game for silly kids. What is important in the song are the words: "To the circle of St. Michael, all bring a box of honey." We all bring something to Mass, whether it is joy, thanksgiving, hope, forgiveness, or faith. These are positive things. However, negative things can also be brought to the Mass, such as remorse, sadness, anger, a broken relationship, physical or psychological ailments, or depression. We celebrants must keep in mind what is in the hearts and minds of those out there and do our best to elicit the joy of the Gospel and Christian living as well as to reach out to those in sorrow, worry, or anxiety.

Latinos are emotional and feel the joys and tribulations of life deeply. Somehow, the liturgy has to connect with those emotions. No one, no matter how little they think they are bringing to Mass, should feel left out.

At the time of St. Paul, there were people who were excluded from the Eucharist. In 1 Corinthians 11, St. Paul reprimands the Christians of Corinth for not sharing the meal that was held in those days in celebration of the Eucharist. I once had a Scripture professor who said, "I often thank God that the Christians of Corinth were misbehaving. If it had not been for them, we would not have St. Paul's understanding and teaching on the Eucharist."

After describing the institution of the Lord's Supper, St. Paul admonishes them with the words, "Whoever, therefore, eats the bread or drinks the cup of the Lord in an unworthy manner will be answerable for the body and blood of the Lord. Examine yourselves, and only then eat of the bread and drink of the cup" (1 Cor. 11:27–28). It seems that what he regards as receiving the Eucharist unworthy is ignoring and forgetting about those who are hungry and feel left out.

Earlier in the book, I describe how my grandparents were forbidden from entering the church to attend Mass but had to look through the windows. Nowadays this does not happen as far as I know, but groups of people who attend our churches for Catholic worship can feel left out when their presence and pastoral needs are not considered.

The preaching, the music, the art, the environment, and a welcoming ambience should be in place at all our liturgies in order that all people feel at home. We should ask the question, Does everyone feel at home, especially the poor and those who are not as well dressed as everyone else? Another question could be whether families with several small children are welcomed even when the children could be a distraction for others. Are the issues addressed in homilies pertinent to the lives and socioeconomic levels of the poor as well as people who are better off? Are parishes truly family-friendly, and do they welcome even those who do not reflect the traditional nuclear family, including single mothers or fathers with their children? Are people who are disabled or who bring their disabled children or relatives accommodated in ways that make them feel part of the congregation? Are they invited to take leadership roles in the liturgy as readers, cantors, and ushers?

There are also the canonically disabled, those who have divorced and remarried civilly and who, because of their status, are not allowed to receive communion. Many of those who are born and baptized Catholic have left the church because of their marital situation. Some do decide to go through the annulment process, but for many Latinos, this process is very strange and new as well as expensive. Many have the impression that annulments are for the rich, the powerful, and those with influence in the church. Many find it an almost impossible process, sometimes because of the paperwork, or because of what is perceived as an intrusion into their private lives by strangers. Pope Francis has streamlined the annulment process and has asked that, wherever possible, fees be removed.

What in the United States is referred to as cohabitation, that is, those couples who live together but are unmarried, in the Latino world could be called *amancebados*. Some of those who cohabit do so without a commitment and may or may not eventually wed. But the *amancebados* of the Latino world are often poor people who are committed to one another but cannot afford the traditional Latino wedding that includes a church celebration and a fiesta with a meal and a dance. Some parishes with great numbers of Latinos sometimes prepare several couples for marriage together and then have a communal wedding celebration in the church, followed by a big fiesta. Pastors must do all that is possible to *regulate* those who are not married in the church in order that they participate in the liturgical life of the church.

Newcomers seeking the sacraments encounter conditions or requirements unheard of in their native countries. Some parishes still insist that people register and use envelopes for church collections before they or their children can receive the sacraments. We know that some of our diocesan or parish policies go beyond the requirements of Canon Law itself. When we reflect on these situations, we can better understand why so many people resort to popular religion instead of accepting the official worship of the church.

The Catholic Challenge:
Connecting Life and Worship

As of this writing, the long-awaited Spanish version of the Roman Missal for use in the United States is not yet available. When released, it will be unique, inasmuch as it will include the Masses for all patronal feasts for all the countries where Spanish is the primary language.

The new translations of the Roman Missal include changes in the Rite of Dismissal suggested by Pope Benedict XVI. These new texts bring fresh and needed clarity to what happens at the end of the celebration of the mysteries of the Eucharist. They connect what we have just done in the Eucharist with what we live out as missionary disciples, a term introduced, no doubt, through the influence of the now Pope Francis at the Fifth General Conference of the Bishops of Latin America held in Aparecida, Brazil, in 2007. What is of great importance to these brief formulas is that they remind us of our central identity: that we are believers in Jesus Christ and follow him as missionary disciples. This is a challenge not only for Latinos but for everyone.

Before I share and explain the new dismissal texts, I will explain what the concluding document of Aparecida says about the Eucharist: "It is the privileged place of the disciples' encounter with Jesus Christ. With this sacrament, Jesus attracts us to himself and makes us enter into his dynamism towards God and towards neighbor. There is a close connection between the three dimensions of the Christian vocation: BELIEVING, CELEBRATING, AND LIVING the mystery of Jesus Christ. . . . The faithful must live in faith in the centrality of the paschal mystery of Christ through the Eucharist so that their whole life is increasingly Eucharistic life. The Eucharist . . . is at the same time the inextinguishable source of missionary drive" (Aparecida Concluding Document, no. 251).

It is interesting to note that at the end of the Aparecida Conference, every bishops' conference in Latin America and the Caribbean was asked to conduct a continental mission, a *Gran Misión,* which would have no end but which would continue indefinitely. The idea of this mission was to emphasize that the church is always in mission.

Actually, the church exists because it has a mission, the mission to evangelize the world and give it cause to rejoice in the saving events initiated and fulfilled by Jesus Christ. The missionary activity of the church, says the Second Vatican Council, comes from its very nature; "according to the plan of the Father, it has its origin in the mission of the Son and the

Holy Spirit" (*Ad Gentes* no. 2). The Son was sent by the Father to reconcile the world to himself. Jesus Christ is the first missioner, the "one Sent" according to St. John's Gospel. Christ, in turn, sent the Holy Spirit to exercise his saving influence and to promise the spread of the church. What we are sent to do at the end of the Mass is to be part of the epic story of God's plan of salvation. We are reminded that we are links in an unbreakable chain that has its beginning with the mission of the first apostles. This is the continual challenge of Pope Francis that we live up to our call and our existence as missionary disciples, that is, we go out, especially to the people at the margins.

Just what are these new formulas? They are as follows:

GO FORTH, THE MASS IS ENDED.
GO AND ANNOUNCE THE GOSPEL OF THE LORD.
GO IN PEACE, GLORIFYING THE LORD BY YOUR LIFE.

Our response is, "THANKS BE TO GOD."

The inspiration for these texts comes directly from His Holiness Pope Benedict XVI. This is what he wrote in the 2007 post-synodal apostolic exhortation, *Sacramentum Caritatis*:

I would like to comment briefly on the observations of the Synod Fathers regarding the dismissal at the end of the Eucharistic celebration. After the blessing, the deacon or the priest dismisses the people with the words: *Ite, missa est*. These words help us to grasp the relationship between the Mass just celebrated and the mission of Christians in the world. In antiquity, *missa* simply meant "dismissal." However, in Christian usage, it gradually took on a deeper meaning.

The word "dismissal" has come to imply a "mission." These few words succinctly express the missionary nature of the Church. The people of God might be helped to understand more clearly this essential dimension of the Church's life, taking the dismissal as a starting point. In this context, it might also be helpful to provide new texts, duly approved, for the prayer over the people and the final blessing, in order to make this connection clear." (no. 51)

The Latino Appreciation and Custom of Farewell

Related to the theme of dismissal at the end of Mass is the Latino appreciation of saying good-bye. *Adios* is taken most seriously among Latinos. Even the word *adios* means, "Go forth to God." A common gesture is for those leaving home, whether for school, work, or a social event, to ask for their parents' blessing. This is also true when a child, of whatever age, goes on a journey. It is considered most important for the children to be present when a parent is dying and to say farewell, and, if possible, receive a final blessing from the father or mother.

The *quinceañera,* the celebration of a young woman's fifteenth birthday, is a farewell to childhood and a welcoming to womanhood. It is common to see parents give a blessing of farewell to their children as they begin the wedding ceremony. At funerals, the farewell can be intensely and deeply felt; we have to remind the family that, yes, there is sadness in leave-taking; however, there is rejoicing in heaven. There, the soul sees God and is reunited with those who have gone before.

There is a secular song called "*La Golondrina*" ("The Swallow") that is sung in farewell settings. For those of us who are old enough to remember watching the televised closing ceremonies of the 1968 Olympics in Mexico City, hundreds of *mariachis* played and sang this song to the departing athletes and visitors from all over the world. The Mexicans wept.

A dónde irá, veloz y fatigada

La golondrina que de aquí se va
O, si en el viento se hallará extraviada
Buscando abrigo y no lo encontrará
Dejé también mi patriaidolatra, esa mansión
Que me miró nacer,

Mi vida es hoy errante y angustiada
Y ya no puedo a mi mansión volver.
Junto a mi lecho le pondré su nido
En donde pueda la estación pasar
También yo estoy en la región perdido
¡Oh! Cielo santo y sin poder volar.
Ave querida amada peregrina
Mi corazón al tuyo estrecharé

Oiré tu canto, tierna golondrina

Recordaré mi patria y lloraré.

Where is it going, so fast and so tired

The swallow that flies away
She may be caught in the wind and lost.
Looking for a harbor, which she will not find
I, too, left my adored fatherland, that mansion that witnessed my birth,

My life is now aimless and full of anguish.
I will never be able to return to my mansion.
I will make a nest for it near my bed
Where it might survive the tempest;
I, too, find myself lost in this storm,
Oh! Holy Heaven, without being able to fly.
Beloved bird, cherished pilgrim,
I will stretch my heart out to you;
I will hear your song, endearing swallow,
I will recall my fatherland, and I, too, will weep.

As the now St. John Paul II was flying out of Mexico City after his first visit there in 1979, people rushed to their rooftops with mirrors to flash at the departing plane. The pope's plane circled the sky over the city. The pope would return four more times to his beloved Mexico.

There are two beautiful *Guadalupan* songs of farewell often sung at the end of Mass. One is *"Adios, Oh Virgen de Guadalupe."*

Adios, Oh Virgen de Guadalupe,
Adios, Oh Madre del Salvador.
Desde que niño nombrarte supe,
Eres mi vida, eres mi vida, mi solo amor.

The other is *"Adios Reina del Cielo."*

Adios, Reina del cielo
Madre del Salvador
Adios, O Madre mía,
Adios, adios, adios

Perhaps these experiences can help develop a catechesis to form people to appreciate the Dismissal Rite in the Mass.

The Symbol of the Cosmic Spiral— Brings In, Sends Out

For me, the Eucharist has two forces of energy: one that summons us to the center and the other that sends us forth like the image of the spiral. The shape of the spiral reminds me of the Eucharist, which brings us together to the center of our Christian selves, and that is, of course, the person of Jesus Christ. At the moment of dismissal at the end of the Eucharist, we are sent forth to the ends of the earth, the way the apostles were sent on the mission to set the world ablaze with the Word of the Gospel and the powerful spirit of the resurrection.

It is fascinating how often the spiral appears in nature and in ancient and indigenous folklore. Spirals show up in Celtic art, indigenous petroglyphs in both North America and Latin America, the Nazca earthworks in Peru, in Arabic architecture, Japanese rock gardens, Hindu spiritual texts, Australian aboriginal paintings, and African art.

At the monumental French Cathedral at Chartres and at spiritual centers around the world, the image of the spiral forms the shape of the labyrinth. We see it in the form of hurricanes, tornadoes, and waterspouts. We find it in the early growth of ferns, in the pattern of leaves growing on certain plants, and in the formation of the nautilus shell. How can we forget that our tiny planet is whirling around space among millions of stars that make up our galaxy, the Milky Way, which moves like a colossal spiral?

The spiral is all around us, as if it were seeking our attention to tell us something. It has been associated with cycles of time; the seasons; the cycles of birth, growth, death, and then rebirth again.

At the Eucharist, Christians return again and again to the source and font of the saving waters of baptism, and our flame of faith is rekindled that we might set the world on fire with divine love, challenging the world to become the place where the kingdom of justice and peace will take root and flourish. Thus, the spiral can remind us that we are channels of God's love, of his life, of his grace, and of his joy.

Sacramentum Caritatis

In *Sacramentum Caritatis*, Pope Benedict makes the strong plea, words that appear to be taken directly from the Aparecida document, that the most holy mystery of the Eucharist "needs to be firmly believed, devoutly celebrated, and intensely lived in the Church. . . . The offering of our lives, our fellowship with the whole community of believers and our solidarity with all men and women are essential aspects of that spiritual worship, holy and pleasing to God (cf. Rom 12:1), which transforms every aspect of our human existence, to the glory of God." The pope exhorts "the lay faithful to find ever anew in the sacrament of Christ's love the energy needed to make their lives an authentic sign of the presence of the risen Lord" (no. 94).

All who claim any sort of expertise in the liturgy must read and study this document, for in it Pope Benedict places such things as the church's work for justice and peace in the context of the Eucharist. Communion with Christ is also communion with all those to whom he gives Himself—which means, everybody in the world. Once we recognize this connection, this recognition, we are led to commit ourselves to transform unjust structures and to restore respect for the dignity of all men and women, created in God's image and likeness. When we respond in this way, "the Eucharist becomes in life what it signifies in its celebration." The pope makes the strong plea that the church "cannot and must not remain on the sidelines in the struggle for justice" (no. 89).

The Holy Father is saying some profound and very challenging things here—that the Eucharist reaches out to the ends of the world in order to save it. This is totally in keeping with what is prominent in the Eucharistic prayers.

In the third Eucharistic prayer, the priest says, "May this Sacrifice of our reconciliation, we pray, O Lord, advance the peace and salvation of all the world."

In the Eucharistic Prayer for Reconciliation II we pray,

May he make your Church a sign of unity and an instrument of your peace among all people. . . . Bring us to share with those who have died in your friendship the unending banquet of unity in a new heaven and a new earth, where the fullness of your peace will shine forth.

In the Eucharistic Prayer for Use in Masses for Various Needs I, we pray in the preface: "By the word of your Son's Gospel you have brought together one Church from every people, tongue and nation, and, having filled her with life by the power of your Spirit, you never cease through her to gather the whole human race into one." Yes, at Mass, we Catholics say some pretty daring things!

The Holy Father goes on to call the Eucharist "a mystery of liberation" and, in the light of this, urges all the faithful to be true promoters of peace and justice. "All who partake of the Eucharist must commit themselves to peacemaking in our world scarred by violence and war, and today in particular, by terrorism, economic corruption and sexual exploitation" (no. 89).

He addresses the unfortunate effects of globalization, which has provoked "inequalities that cry out to heaven," and that it is impossible to remain silent before the "distressing images of huge camps throughout the world of displaced persons and refugees, who are living in makeshift conditions . . . Are these human beings not our brothers and sisters? Do their children not come into the world with the same legitimate expectations of happiness as other children?"

He makes the point that less than half of the huge sums spent worldwide on armaments would be more than sufficient to liberate the immense masses of the poor from destitution. He again connects these challenges with the Eucharist reminding us that it is the "sacrament of charity" (no. 90).

With these powerful statements, it is quite understandable why he wanted new formulas for the Dismissal Rite, which would underscore the need to extend the gift and challenge of Eucharist to the world.

Utilizing the Gifts and Meeting the Challenge of Latino Catholics in Worship

Formation of liturgical ministers is one of the most important concerns of a parish. If we are going to have an impact on the liturgical life of this country from the Latino perspective, then we must be alert and eager to contribute to the formation of liturgical ministers—all of them. I am thinking of the formation of priests, deacons, acolytes, lectors, extraordinary Eucharistic ministers, musicians, creators of environment and art, and everyone in any way who is taking part in the leadership or service of the worshiping assembly.

I am referring here not simply to the development of skills for the practical implementation of good liturgy but also to a deeper theological and cultural understanding of Latino religious tradition and liturgical needs. For this to take place, I think we must continue to focus on the training of professional liturgical thinkers.

We have not yet begun to fill the enormous gaps that exist in the world of theological academia with regard to the enculturation of liturgy and, in particular, of the enculturation of Latino liturgy into the life of the church.

I dream of Latino American teachers of theology at the great theological centers in North America and Europe, including the great universities in Rome. Until this happens, our efforts will be seen as unprofessional, and we will be seen as ethno-centrists. In other words, we will not be taken seriously until we have spokespersons at the highest academic levels. I also dream of more Latino architects, religious artists, and church interior designers to create an atmosphere that relates to Latino culture.

It goes without saying that the priests, in spite of the consultative structures that may be in place, still control what happens in liturgy, especially in the sanctuary. This should point to the absolute necessity of bringing our concerns for Latino liturgy to the forefront of the formation of future priests. Latinos are present in every diocese in the United States. Their liturgical needs must be met as much as those of any other group.

Our country is becoming increasingly Spanish speaking. The church is becoming more Spanish speaking. We need to maintain the pressure for the preparation of those involved in liturgy to know Spanish. Equally important is the familiarity with and embrace of the rich religious traditions of our peoples and for them to recognize the multicultural Latino presence in this country. It will also be important for them to be aware of the various degrees of participation in the church. Similar to other groups, some Latinos are more *churched* than others. I daresay the majority have received the two sacraments of Baptism and First Communion, and that is about it. The majority have yet to be fully initiated into the church.

We have to do something with the fear that many of our Latino peoples have toward pastoral leaders, especially bishops and priests. I am concerned that we have far too many in church leadership positions who are intolerant of anyone who is different and whose ecclesiology or faith expressions are different from their own. This can be true of native US priests, as well as foreign priests, who can have an elitist regard of themselves and their ideas of worship. Those who are successful in making the cross-cultural transition—and thanks be to God, there are many of these—are to be admired.

The Music of Fiesta

Music has always been an integral part of all of liturgy. Even in the letters of Paul, we find semblances of worship songs such as the hymn to Christ in the letter to the Philippians 2:5–11. It is also striking that Jesus himself on the night of his betrayal, on the eve of his Passion and death, sang the *hallel* songs with the apostles. In Matthew 26:30 we read, "When they had sung the hymn, they went out to the Mount of Olives." It can almost be said that Jesus sang on the way to his death.

For Latinos, it is most appropriate for singing to be part of prayer and worship. Latinos everywhere are noted for their love of music; it is part of their day-to-day living.

As in many other cultures, the first music we hear is usually that of our mothers singing us lullabies. In my childhood, I remember hearing the music of my family and friends. What I remember foremost is the music of *la acordión y la guitarra*. The guitar probably had its origins in the Mediterranean world, particularly in Spain. The accordion came to the Mexican world both in Texas and in northern Mexico through the Germans and Eastern Europeans such as the Czechs and the Poles. This was the beginning of the rich musical genre called *Tejano* music.

The same can be said for Latinos in other places, all who have rich musical backgrounds. Those that come to mind are Caribbean music, with its African influences, and the many traditions from Latin America: Colombia, the Andes, Brazil, Argentina, and Chile. What is exciting to hear is sacred music developed especially since the Second Vatican Council incorporating the rhythms and melodious style of Latin America.

Here in the United States, Latino pastoral musicians are numerous. They have contributed a new treasure of Spanish hymnology. The hymnal *Flor y Canto* in use throughout the

United States is filled with music that has come forth from the Latino faith in the United States. It is commendable that these musicians come together on a regular basis for the National Hispanic Pastoral Musicians Conference. At the conference, composers share their music among themselves and with the gathered people of God. Some of the new compositions are bilingual and can be sung in bilingual Masses.

Much attention needs to be given to Latino pastoral musicians. Many of these do not know how to read music; it is all played by ear. Therefore, we see throughout the country variations of the same hymn, which I am sure would not be acceptable to the composers. Therefore, it is incumbent for pastoral musicians to do all they can to learn to read the music as well as be reminded often of their importance in leading the community in worship. They may need to be repeatedly told that they are not performers but those who lead the rest of the congregation in singing.

As with other liturgical ministers, there is an absolute need for these musicians to develop their spirituality and establish a strong community spirit among themselves. Unfortunately, there can be divisions and tensions among the members of a choir. Retreats or days of recollection can be necessary in order to make sure not only that their music is beautiful but also that the communal relationship is nourished. When there is division within a choir and the people know about it, it is less than commendable and may even border on scandal.

When he was in Houston, Dr. John Francis Burke worked as music director for a bilingual parish, and unfortunately the parish suffered from lack of unity among Spanish-speaking and English-speaking communities. Dr. Burke decided to start with the choirs. The way he attempted to resolve the problem was to have both choirs, English and Spanish, practice on the same evening. The English choir would arrive at 7:00 p.m.

and would practice for half an hour. At 7:30 p.m., the Spanish choir would arrive, and both choirs would practice together, especially bilingual hymns. At 8:00 p.m., the English choir would leave and the Spanish choir would practice alone for another half hour. This helped to bring the two communities together and to appreciate one another's music.

Earlier in this book, in the chapter on catechesis or handing on the faith, I referred to St. Augustine and his advice to catechists. In order to communicate the Gospel effectively, St. Augustine writes that one has to teach, captivate, and convince. This can also be said about the challenge to communicate by pastoral musicians, since by their music ministry they are, in the words of Aparecida, disciples and missionaries.

Pastoral musicians hand on the truth of Jesus Christ through their music. For this reason, they ought to know the truth and the person of Jesus Christ, and this requires a deep understanding and love of the truth they communicate. According to Augustine, we are called to set aflame the love of God and the love of neighbor in the hearts of others. When a choir sings, it maintains the attention of its hearers through its music. This could be called the captivating moment. The convincing happens due to the witness of the ministers of music, the love they show in their music for the mysteries of the faith, and where the witness of their Christian lives shines.

As a mariachi musician, Salvador Hernandez told me, *"Nosotros, los músicos, tenemos que hacer que la gente se siente bonita por medio de la música"* (We musicians have the task to make the people feel beautiful about themselves through our music). That is why musicians have to do their very best to sing with all their hearts, pay attention to every word they sing, and try to enter into the mind and heart of the composer.

St. Augustine also reminds us that we must sing with our hearts full of joy. This joy has its source in the love that we have for the truth we are transmitting. Contemporary choirs nowadays often sit or stand near the altar, and people are watching them throughout the liturgy. I beg the choir members to show their joy with smiles when singing, especially when the hymn is about the joy of God's love.

Our joy is a sign that we have brought the spirit of fiesta into our worship.

Chapter 11

The Francis Effect on Latinos

My theological studies as a seminarian were in Toronto, Canada, at St. Basil's Seminary, and Mexico City, at the Seminario Conciliar de México, the seminary for the Archdiocese of Mexico City.

The summer of 1964, after our first year of theology in Toronto, a fellow Basilian seminarian, Robert (Bob) Power, C.S.B., and I were sent to work at the mission the Basilians had in the outskirts of Mexico City, San Juan de Aragón, not far from the Shrine of Our Lady of Guadalupe.

Going from the comforts of a North American seminary and the city of Toronto to an impoverished Third World community of San Juan de Aragón was a daunting experience. Water was scarce, so we showered only once a week. Only two meals were served each day; I remember often eating only a banana for dinner. It was the rainy season, so the unpaved streets of the pueblo (town) were mostly mud. At the time, the people of the town had farm animals such as cows, pigs, horses, donkeys, and chickens. The whole town smelled like a stable. Each morning we awakened to the sound of donkeys braying. Sometimes some of these animals would wander into the church with the people.

What made up for all this was the faith of the people. Their poverty and simple way of life identified them strongly with their notion of Jesus, together with his mother, Mary, whom they saw as poor and their companions on their pilgrimage of life. What was also most helpful was the team of Basilians and the Mexican community of sisters, the Missionary Catechists of the Hearts of Jesus and Mary. Their passion for bringing the joy and consolation of the Gospel was ever evident.

When Bob and I returned to Toronto after our summer in Mexico, we wanted to minister with the Basilian team in San Juan de Aragón after ordination. To prepare for this, we asked our superiors if we could study the rest of our theology in Mexico City. We argued that since some Basilian seminarians were being sent each year to study theology in Paris, France, why couldn't the two of us study in Mexico City? Our superiors thought it was a great idea, and in January 1965, Bob and I moved to Mexico City.

Adjusting from the religious community of St. Basil's Seminary to a diocesan seminary in another country was a painful culture shock. Yet we made lifelong friends, improved our Spanish, learned the cultures of Mexico in depth, and saw and felt the world and the church through the eyes and the hearts of the Mexican people. Even though it was difficult, it was a rich moment of grace.

One of our Mexican seminarian friends was a professional artist, and before Christmas break, he gave me a small watercolor to take to my mother in Texas. It was a stylized Madonna, the artist's version of the Blessed Virgin Mary as a Japanese woman.

I wrapped it as best I could and gave it to my mother. She was happy that I had brought her something, but when it was unwrapped, she looked at the picture and asked, "Who's that?"

I said, "It's the Blessed Virgin."

She responded, "It doesn't look like the Blessed Virgin!"

I tried to explain that our Blessed Mother appears to people around the world dressed like the women of the places she visits. She appeared in France, Portugal, and Mexico dressed like the women there. I further explained that she was of Jewish origins, born and raised in Galilee, where she lived.

My mother's reaction was, "Is that what they're teaching you in the seminary? Everyone knows she is Mexican, Our Lady of Guadalupe!"

I asked her, "How about St. Joseph?"
"Oh, yes, son, he was el Señor San José; he, too, was a Mexican!"
"What about the apostles; do you think they were Mexican?"
"Of course, San Pedro, San Pablo, Santiago, they were all Mexican!"
Then I asked, "What about San Judas Iscariote, the betrayer?"
"Oh no," she answered. "He was something else!"

*   *   *

Reflecting on the people's spirituality in both Mexico and with my family in Texas, I saw a commonality. The world of the sacred was not far from them. I also learned to recognize that their notions of faith were as profound as those of any theology professor in the seminary. The popular religion that I witnessed in them was not anything to look down on; it offered a glimpse of heaven on earth. No wonder Pope Francis has such respect and admiration for the faith of the *pueblo*.

Cardinal Jorge Bergoglio was elected pope on the evening of March 13, 2013. Immediately after his election, it was clear that his style would be much different from other popes. First, he chose the name Francis, the first in the history of the papacy to take that name. It was his way of indicating that the poor would hold a special place in his heart. He decided not to sit on the papal throne when each cardinal came to congratulate him, and he stood to deemphasize his new supreme status. When he went to the balcony overlooking the Piazza of St. Peter's, he did not wear the rich and showy garb traditionally worn by popes when greeting the faithful; neither did he wear a bejeweled golden pectoral cross, but rather the same simple iron cross he had worn as the Cardinal Archbishop of Buenos Aires.

His first words to the people gathered before him were, "Good evening!" Of course, the crowd roared with joy and laughter. He asked the people to pray in silence for his predecessor, Benedict XVI, and for himself.

Instead of riding in a Mercedes limousine, he rode the bus with the rest of the cardinals to the boardinghouse where they were staying during the Conclave. The next day he went to the hotel where he had been staying before the Conclave to get his suitcase and to pay his bill. Later he decided he would not reside at the Papal Palace with its hallways and meeting rooms richly decorated in the Renaissance style; he would live at Casa Santa Marta, the boardinghouse inside the Vatican. He says daily Mass with the people who live and work there and eats with the other residents.

As he was leaving Casa Santa Marta on one of his first mornings there, he walked out of the front door and saw a Swiss guard standing by the doorway. He greeted the young man and asked what he was doing there. The guard answered, "I have been guarding you, Your Holiness."

"And how long have you been here, young man?" the pope asked.

"Oh, Your Holiness, I have been here all night!"

Pope Francis then asked him, "And you have been standing all night?"

"Yes," the guard answered.

"Well," the pope responded, "I will bring you a chair so you can sit."

The guard quickly said, "But we are not allowed to sit while we are guarding you."

The pope found him a chair and told the guard to sit. He said, "I am the pope, you sit! By the way, have you eaten?"

"No," answered the guard, "We're not allowed to eat."

Again the pope said, "Well, I'm the pope, you will eat the food I will bring you!"

The pope went back into the residence and brought the guard a sandwich.

"Here, eat!"

It was in this way that Pope Francis would impress the world with his style of humility, service, mercy, and simplicity. Prior to his election to the papacy, Cardinal Bergoglio said, "Thinking of the next pope, he must be a man who, from the contemplation and adoration of Jesus Christ, helps the Church to go out to the existential peripheries which will help her to become a fruitful mother, revitalized by the 'sweet and comforting joy of evangelizing.'"

Reaching Out to Those at the Margins

When Pope Francis speaks of existential peripheries, he is speaking of the people who live on the margins. He often invites us to reach out to the peripheries where no one goes: "Come out of the caves, leave the sacristies." He calls priests, bishops, and all of the church to come out of their personal comfort zone or from the circle of nice people, and to be close to all. That is what Jesus did, spending time with the blind man on the road, the leper, and the sinful woman.

Reaching out to people on the margins is the inspiration for this book. Pope Francis in February 2015, in a homily for twenty new cardinals, called on the cardinals of the world to avoid becoming a closed caste and instead to imitate Jesus in reaching out to those at the margins. In what could almost be considered a vision statement for his papacy, he said, "We will not find the Lord unless we truly accept the marginalized!" Francis said. "Truly the Gospel of the marginalized is where our credibility is found and revealed!" (Mass in St. Peter's Basilica).

The pontiff laid out a vision for the prelates of a church that not only welcomes all but also goes out looking for every excluded person, especially those who are hungry, thirsty, and naked.

Pope Francis says the Roman Catholic Church must be open and welcoming, whatever the costs. He asks the church to reach out to all who are rejected by society and the church.

"He Is One of Us!"

There are differing analyses with regard to the visit of Pope Francis to the United States in September 2015. For sure, Latinos who left the church or religion altogether are not flocking back to Mass. What is generally accepted is that those who regularly practice their Catholic faith are becoming stronger in their beliefs and practices. It is also fair to say that the full impact of Pope Francis on Latinos will happen over time and not just in the immediate aftermath of his visit.

There are many reasons why Latinos who love the church, who want to see it grow and be successful in its evangelization efforts, are encouraged by the strong influence of Pope Francis. He is the first pope from south of the equator and from Latin America. Latinos readily and truthfully say, "He is one of us!"

The pope's visit to Mexico was especially meaningful to US Latinos, not only for Mexicans and Mexican–Americans living here but for all Latinos. Traveling from the southern border of Mexico to the northern one symbolized the difficult journey that so many immigrants make in their search for a better life. He accomplished what he set out to do, that is, to be a missionary of hope and peace. His words and gestures of love and understanding deepened the faith and hope in the hearts and minds of Latinos in the United States.

It became very clear that Pope Francis shares the love for Our Lady of Guadalupe with Latinos, and his messages throughout his trip resounded with the reality lived day in and day out in the US among youth, the elderly, the sick, children, and married couples.

Pope Francis's Identity with Immigrants

It is significant that the pope visited Cuba before entering the United States in 2015. As the pope was preparing for his visit, the Vatican Secretary of State, Cardinal Pietro Parolin, said the pope would be arriving in the US as a migrant. Jorge Mario Bergoglio is a son of immigrants. His own country, Argentina, like the United States, is a nation of immigrants. Argentina is the nation most like Europe in all of Latin America. One only has to observe the surnames, which are generally Italian or German as well as Spanish.

Buenos Aires was, together with New York, a main destination for the vast transatlantic migration in the latter nineteenth and early twentieth centuries. In the 1880s, 1.5 million people entered Argentina, and between 1890 and 1914, the numbers reached 4.3 million. Over a million Italians and some 800,000 Spanish made new lives there, as well as others from Eastern Europe and the Middle East. Many of these were wealthy business and professional people, but there were those of lower economic status, such as the Bergoglio family, who were lower middle class.[1]

In his address to the US Congress, the pope called for legislation favoring immigration. He was especially concerned about the thousands traveling north "in search of a better life for themselves and their loved ones, in search of greater opportunities. Is this not what we want for our own children? We must not be taken aback by their numbers, but rather, view them as persons, seeing their faces and listening to their stories, trying to respond as best we can to their situation. To respond in a way which is always humane, just, and fraternal."

Immigration reform advocates and others do not believe the pope's talk to Congress will immediately lead to immigration

---

[1] Austen Ivereigh, *The Great Reformer: Francis and the Making of a Radical Pope* (New York: Henry Holt, 2014), 8–9.

reform. Jean Atkinson, executive director of the Catholic Legal Immigration Network, Inc., said she hopes people who watched the speech will help change lawmakers' minds over time. "I'm hoping that people listening around the country will reach out to their members of Congress and say this is something that needs to be addressed."[2]

Hope for the Latino Poor

Latinos suffering from poverty, specifically seasonal workers who are undocumented immigrants living in the shadows of our society, are encouraged by seeing a pope so strong in his defense of the poor. Minutes after his election as pope, a close friend of his, Cardinal Claudio Hummes, approached him and reminded him not to forget the poor. Cardinal Bergoglio said it was at that moment that he thought of Francis, the saint of the poor, to take as his papal name.

Yet, Pope Francis's concern for the poor did not come at his election, but rather had been in his heart and mind all the years of his priesthood. He was strongly influenced by the documents of the Second Vatican Council and by its application to Latin America in Medellín, Colombia, in 1968. The declaration by the Latin American Bishops Confederation gave the church on the continent its own distinctive voice, above all, by articulating what it called the preferential option for the poor. In 2010, Archbishop Bergoglio explained what this meant to him:

> The option for the poor comes from the first centuries of Christianity. It is the Gospel itself. If you were to read one of the sermons of the first fathers of the

---

[2] Erin Kelly, "Pope's Immigration Message Draws Praise, Criticism from Advocacy Groups," *USA Today*, September 24, 2015, http://www.usatoday.com/story/news/2015/09/24/pope-immigration-congress-speech-advocates-tussle/72699836/.

Church, from the second or third centuries, about how you should treat the poor, you would say it was Maoist or Trotskyist. The Church has always had the honor of this preferential option for the poor. It has always considered the poor to be the treasure of the Church. During the (third-century) persecution of the deacon Lawrence, who was the administrator of the diocese (of Rome), they told him to bring all the treasures of the Church. A few days later, he appeared with a throng of poor people and said, "These are the treasure of the Church." At the Second Vatican Council the Church was redefined as the People of God and this idea really took off at the Second Conference of the Latin-American bishops in Medellin."[3]

The bishops of Argentina embraced Medellín and adapted it to Argentina in their 1969 declaration of San Miguel. It embraced the new direction set by Medellín, calling for a church that "honors the poor, loves them, defends them and embraces their cause while offering a mea culpa for the way the Church often appears wealthy."[4] At the same time, the document rejected Marxism as "alien not only to Christianity, but also to the spirit of our people." It saw the people, *el pueblo*, as active agent of its own history and asserted, "The activity of the Church should not only be oriented towards the people but also primarily derived from the people." This vision identified the church with the ordinary people as the subjects of their own history rather than as a class engaged in a social struggle with other classes. According to his biographer, Austen Ivereigh, Bergoglio shared the vision of San Miguel.[5]

---

[3] Ivereigh, *The Great Reformer*, 94–95.

[4] Ibid., 95.

[5] Ibid.

Pope Francis's Affirmation
of Popular Religiosity

Pope Francis has an incredible love and respect for the people's religiosity. In Chapter 8, I described and gave an analysis of the spirituality of the Latino people. The present pope's profound and lifelong appreciation of the people's approach to holiness resonates with the prominent place popular religion has in the hearts and souls of the Latino people.

The spirituality of Jorge Bergoglio, the child of Italian immigrants, was influenced deeply by popular piety. According to Austen Ivereigh, the single greatest childhood influence on him was his grandmother Rosa, with whom he spent most of his first five years. She and grandfather Giovanni made sure Jorge did not lose his Italian culture and religion. Rosa shared her devotion to the saints with young Jorge, taught him the Rosary, and on Good Friday, she took the grandchildren to see the crucified Christ and told them he would rise on Easter Sunday. Jorge's parents continued the responsibility of handing on their Catholic faith by word and example.[6]

The Catholic people's spirituality in Argentina helped in the maintenance of the faith and handing it on to their children and grandchildren. In the early twentieth century, church institutions, such as schools, churches, seminaries, convents, and hospitals, were built in the cities of Buenos Aires and Córdoba. Outside of those metropolitan areas, the rural poor had little contact with the official church. Popular religion, which for Jorge Bergoglio was a sign of an evangelized culture, maintained the faith of the poor and was the means whereby they handed it on to their children and grandchildren, especially through their devotions and faith traditions.

---

[6]   Ibid., 13–14.

In 1976, Father Bergoglio became the rector of the *Colegio Máximo*, the flagship educational institution of the Jesuits in Argentina. As rector, Father Bergoglio was the director of the faculties of philosophy and theology, which placed him in charge of the formation of close to one hundred Jesuit students. This number would double by the time he stepped down in 1986.

In the reorganization of the studies of philosophy and theology, emphasis was given to the *teología del pueblo* (theology of the people), with its emphasis on popular religiosity. Father Bergoglio, inspired by the first Jesuit missionaries in South America, made the option for the poor, expressed in manual labor, hands-on pastoral care, and a deep respect for popular culture and religion. He encouraged respect for the religiosity of pilgrimages, shrines, and devotions. In this way, his students would become enculturated into the lives of God's holy people.

In the pastoral theology classes and meditations, the future pope asked the students to reflect on their experiences and insisted that when they went out to the people, they were not going out to teach but to be taught by the *pueblo fiel* (faithful people). He once wrote, "How difficult it is, and how lonely it can feel, when I realize I must learn from the people their language, their terms of reference, their values, not as a way of polishing my theology but as a new way of being that transforms me."[7]

He encouraged his students to respect and understand popular forms of piety: asking the saints to intercede, praying the rosary, going on pilgrimages, and reverently touching statues. According to one of his theologian friends, Father Bergoglio's idea was that, "Here we have poor people, and because they are poor they rely on faith, and because they have faith, they are our center. Their faith, their culture, their way of expressing their faith—that's what we must value."[8]

---

[7] Ibid., 182.

[8] Ibid.

The appreciation that Jorge Bergoglio has for popular religiosity has, as one of its sources, post–Vatican II documents such as Pope Paul VI's *Evangelii Nuntiandi* and the document of the Third General Conference of the Bishops of Latin America in Puebla, Mexico, in 1979. One of the meaningful messages of Puebla is the recognition that an option for the poor means an option for their distinctive popular culture and religiosity. The future Pope Francis saw Puebla as a breakthrough, for it was now possible to look at Latin America through its own cultural tradition, preserved in the spiritual and religious resources of the ordinary faithful people.

Not everyone was enamored by popular religiosity as taught by Jorge Bergoglio. One of his brother Jesuits wrote,

> You can't believe it; he introduced Argentine Jesuits to popular religiosity. He took them to the barrios, he encouraged a style of popular religiosity among the students, who would go to the chapel at night and touch images! This was something the poor did, the people of the pueblo, something that the Society of Jesus worldwide just does not do. It's just not typical of us.[9]

In 2007, at which time the Archbishop of Buenos Aires was Cardinal Jorge Bergoglio, the Fifth General Conference of the Bishops of Latin America and the Caribbean took place in Aparecida, Brazil. His fellow bishops asked Cardinal Bergoglio to be the chief editor of the final document. One of the unique aspects of the Conference of Aparecida was that we, the delegates, would walk back and forth between the Shrine of Our Lady of Aparecida and our hotel every day. There is a beautiful, elevated walkway between the old shrine and the new one. Our daily journeys enabled us to walk with the

---

[9] Ibid., 193.

ordinary folks, those who had come to Aparecida in pilgrimage. We also held daily Mass at the Basilica of Aparecida in the presence of thousands of pilgrims. This was not purposeful, but it did remind us constantly of the faith of the people.

In his opening address, Pope Benedict XVI paid tribute to the rich and profound popular religiosity, in which we see the soul of the Latin American peoples.

> Love for the suffering Christ, the God of compassion, pardon and reconciliation, the God who loved us to the point of handing himself over for us; love for the Lord present in the Eucharist, the Incarnate God, dead and risen in order to be the bread of life; the God who was close to the poor and to those who suffer; the profound devotion to the most holy Virgin of Guadalupe, the Aparecida, the Virgin invoked under various titles . . . This religiosity is also expressed in devotion to the saints with their patronal feasts, in love for the Pope and the other Pastors, and in love for the Universal Church. . . . All this forms the great mosaic of popular piety, which is the precious treasure of the Catholic Church in Latin America and which must be protected, promoted and, when necessary, purified.[10]

The thinking of Cardinal Bergoglio no doubt influenced the *Concluding Document of Aparecida* in many ways, most notably in the section on popular religiosity (Nos. 258–75). The religion of the Latin American people expresses its Catholic faith. "It is a people's Catholicism."

Aparecida lists the following expressions: the Way of the Cross, patron saint celebrations, novenas, rosaries, processions,

---

[10] *V General Conference of the Bishops of Latin America and the Caribbean, Concluding Document, Aparecida, May 13–15, 2007* (Washington, DC: United States Conference of Catholic Bishops, 2008), 6–7.

dances and songs of religious folklore, affection for the saints and angels, solemn promises, and family prayer. It highlights pilgrimages whereby people journey together toward God. Christ himself becomes a pilgrim and walks among the poor. The decision to make a pilgrimage is already a confession of faith, walking is a true song of hope, and arrival is the encounter of love.

This can be experienced at such places as the Shrine of Our Lady of Luján in Argentina or the Basilica of the Virgin of Aparecida in Brazil. In the United States, people's journey of faith can lead them to the Shrine at Chimayó, in New Mexico, or the Shrine of Our Lady of San Juan del Valle, in Texas. "The pilgrim's gaze rests on an image that symbolizes God's affection and closeness. Love pauses, contemplates mystery, and enjoys it in silence. A living spiritual experience is compressed into that brief moment" (Aparecida no. 259).

In those special moments, people make decisions that mark the rest of their lives and experience the graces of conversion and forgiveness.

The Aparecida document goes on to say that the people's religiosity can lead to the Bible, to greater participation in the sacraments, to greater enjoyment of the Sunday celebration of the Eucharist, and to a better expression of love and solidarity in their lives. It will also provide the means to draw on the rich potential of holiness and social justice encompassed in the mysticism of the people. For many Latino families, it is an indispensable channel of handing on the faith.

The Resonance with the Latino Idea of the Church

Even for those who have not had the opportunity of studying the theology of the church, including the ecclesiology of Vatican II, there is an innate sense of what the church should be. The image that Pope Francis projects resonates strongly in the Latino church.

Pope Francis believes and teaches in the clearest and forceful terms that the church is, first and foremost, the people of God. He affirms the teaching of Vatican II, that the call to holiness is universal, and that all, not just the ordained and those in consecrated life, receive this call at their baptism. Moreover, all who claim to be disciples are also missionaries. From the Latino experience of having received their faith in the family, they can readily accept that faith comes from parents, grandparents, and the extended family, all those in their lives who introduced them to Christ mainly through example.

Pope Francis has placed a huge welcome mat at the door of the church. All are welcomed with joy and a smile. He offers the embrace of mercy and forgiveness. His heart goes out to the poor, the sinner, and the sick. No one is so far out there in the margins that they are excluded from the church he models.

So many Latino families are poor, so many of us come from poor families, so we rejoice when Pope Francis writes in his apostolic exhortation *The Joy of the Gospel* that the poor hold a special place in the church. He refers to the words of Benedict XVI that the church's option for the poor is "implicit in our Christian faith in a God who became poor for us, so as to enrich with his poverty" (*Evangelii Gaudium*, no. 198).

Pope Francis says that he wants a church that is poor and for the poor. "They have much to teach us. Not only do they share in the *sensus fidei*, but in their difficulties they know the suffering Christ. We need to let ourselves be evangelized by them. . . . We are called to find Christ in them, to lend our voice to their causes, but also to be their friends, to listen to them, to speak for them and to embrace the mysterious wisdom which God wishes to share with us through them" (*Evangelii Gaudium* no. 198).

In preaching about Jesus Christ in the here and now to real human beings living in the dirt and grime of life, and in dialogue with those whose beliefs are not our own, priests must know "how to dialogue and to descend into their people's night, into the darkness, but without getting lost." We have the truth that is meant to illuminate the life of each and every person we encounter. We are called to bring the joy, the depth, and the simplicity of the Gospel. In so many words, this is the main message of Pope Francis in his apostolic exhortation *The Joy of the Gospel*.

Those who suffer on account of poverty, who are undocumented, who live in the shadows of society, who leave their beloved homelands for the hard work of farm labor in slaughter and packing houses, dairy farms, and other poorly paid menial tasks, take comfort when the pope refers to the church as a *field hospital*. A field hospital is right in the midst of the battle and the conflicts of life, close to those whose lives need healing. If nothing else, the church offers a compassionate heart, a listening ear, and a place to bring their hurts to God and to Mary, our Mother.

Those who minister in the church must be people of love and mercy and, like the good shepherd in the Scriptures, be there to bind their wounds and hold them close.

Those who minister in the church must be people of love and mercy and, like the good shepherd in the Scriptures, be there to bind their wounds and hold them close, never losing sight that they possess the dynamism of their culture to enrich the rest of society. In his speech in front of Independence Hall in Philadelphia, speaking in Spanish, from the rostrum used by Abraham Lincoln at Gettysburg, Pope Francis connected the theme of religious freedom with the values of the Latino people. He challenged Latinos not to be ashamed of their traditions, rather to contribute their gifts and help renew society from within.

Index